WHATEVER
IT TAKES

WHATEVER IT TAKES

ILLEGAL IMMIGRATION, BORDER SECURITY,
AND THE WAR ON TERROR

CONGRESSMAN

J.D. HAYWORTH

WITH JOSEPH J. EULE

Since 1947
**REGNERY
PUBLISHING, INC.**

An Eagle Publishing Company • Washington, DC

Library of Congress Cataloging-in-Publication Data

Hayworth, J. D. (John D.), 1958–
  Whatever it takes : illegal immigration, border security, and the war on terror / J. D. Hayworth with Joseph J. Eule.
    p. cm.
  Includes bibliographical references and index.

  ISBN 0-89526-028-X

  1. United States—Emigration and immigration—Government policy. 2. Illegal aliens—United States. 3. Border patrols—United States. 4. War on Terrorism, 2001– I. Eule, Joseph J. II. Title.

  JV6483.H386 2006
  325.73—dc22

                                                        2005033948

Published in the United States by

Regnery Publishing, Inc.
One Massachusetts Avenue, NW
Washington, DC 20001
www.regnery.com

Distributed to the trade by
National Book Network
Lanham, MD 20706

Manufactured in the United States of America

10 9 8 7 6 5 4 3 2 1

Books are available in quantity for promotional or premium use. Write to Director of Special Sales, Regnery Publishing, Inc., One Massachusetts Avenue NW, Washington, DC 20001, for information on discounts and terms or call (202) 216-0600.

■ ■ ■

*To my wife, Mary, for her love and
encouragement, and to our children,
Nicole, Hannah, and John Micah,
for what they represent: the future.*

CONTENTS

INTRODUCTION

BY SEAN HANNITY

'VE KNOWN AND ADMIRED Congressman J. D. Hayworth for years as a plain-talking, guts-up conservative who doesn't hesitate to take the fight to the liberals. In just over a decade in Congress, J. D. has become one of the best and most recognized spokesmen of the conservative movement. As a result, he has been a longtime regular on both my radio program and *Hannity & Colmes*.

In recent years, J. D. has become one of the few in Congress pushing a consistent message of enforcing our immigration laws while exposing the folly and dereliction of those who choose to look the other way. J. D. has been one of the most outspoken critics of our weak border security and policies, and his concern for the safety of Americans is well founded. So in April 2005 when I was heading to the Arizona-Mexico border to do some on-scene reporting about the Minuteman Project, I could think of no better companion than J. D.

On the way to the border, we discussed at length the issue of illegal immigration and our shared belief that the problem is getting to the point where, unless we act soon, we could be facing another catastrophe on the order of September 11. By allowing people to cross our borders unchecked, we invite a security risk into our homeland. There is no way of knowing if any—or how many—terrorists have already slipped across our border. We do know that there are more than eight million illegal immigrants in this country, and that they continue to slip through our borders unchecked at an alarming rate. We cannot deny that it would be terribly easy for any terrorist with a modicum of training to cross the border just as easily.

J. D. has written the right book at the right time. The time has come to take control of our borders, increase security, and make sure that every person who crosses our border does so *legally*. We are a nation of immigrants, and we need to make sure that people continue to immigrate to this country according to our rule of law.

J. D. tells the hard truths that many people simply don't want to hear. And trust me when I say that I am all too aware of what J. D. is up against in writing a book like this. I've interviewed Mexican officials who refuse to acknowledge that their countrymen are breaking the law when they cross our border without permission. I've interviewed American officials who make excuse after excuse for why they will not enforce our immigration laws. I've heard all the blather from the open-borders lobby as to why illegal immigration is a *good* thing. The obfuscation, doublespeak, and outright lying are enough to drive you mad.

With this book, J. D. Hayworth sounds the alarm about how illegal immigration threatens the security of our country. J. D. outlines the problem in a way you are unlikely to see in the mainstream media. Now it is up to concerned citizens to demand that the government take the steps that we know will work to stop illegal immigration and protect our nation. Unless something is done, and soon, to get the situation under control, I fear it is only a matter of time before Americans pay another catastrophic price for our inexcusable dereliction in enforcing our immigration laws and controlling our borders. And then it will be too late.

Consider yourself warned. Now read the rest of this book and consider yourself armed...with the truth.

CHAPTER ONE

OVERRUN

"The United States shall guarantee to every State in this Union a Republican Form of Government, and shall protect each of them against Invasion."

—United States Constitution,
Article IV, Section 4

ARIZONA HAS BECOME the new illegal gateway to America. As a congressman representing the fifth congressional district of Arizona, I am all too aware of the chaos caused by the illegal invasion taking place in the state I love and call home.

At *minimum*, almost 4,500 people cross into Arizona illegally *each day* without getting caught, while another 1,500 are apprehended. This means for every illegal alien caught at the border, three make it in, although I have seen some estimates claiming the ratio is as high as one to ten. Try getting odds like that in Vegas.

This invasion has overwhelmed the Border Patrol, devastated communities, ruined the environment, and tested the patience and pocketbooks of Arizona's citizens. And it has become increasingly violent. In one particularly brutal instance, rival gangs of human smugglers had a rolling shoot-out along Interstate 10 in southern Arizona. Four people were killed and several others wounded. Ironically, at the time of the shoot-out, Mexican president Vicente Fox was on his way to Phoenix to talk trade and what he impertinently calls "migration" issues.

The vast majority of illegal border crossers are Mexican. But there is a growing number of what the Border Patrol calls OTMs, or "other than Mexicans." These OTMs come from El Salvador, Brazil, Nicaragua, Venezuela, Afghanistan, Bulgaria, Russia, China, Egypt, Lebanon, Syria, Iran, and Iraq. *Time* magazine estimated that in the first nine months of 2004, as many as 190,000 OTMs "melted into the U.S. population."[1]

And don't think illegal immigration is a problem only for border states. In the blue-collar town of Danbury, Connecticut, about 20 percent of the town's population (75,000) is estimated to be illegal. The situation is so out of control that town officials found thirty cots in the basement of one home, each being rented for five dollars a night. Danbury mayor Mark Boughton told FOX News, "In terms of our social services, this presents a tremendous strain, particularly on quality of life of our neighborhoods, our schools, our health care system."[2] He wanted state police officers deputized as federal immigration officers to deal with the problem.

Here in Arizona, we can feel Danbury's pain—and then some. A June 2004 study by the Federation for American Immigration Reform (FAIR) estimated that the cost of illegal immigration to Arizona taxpayers comes to about *$1.6 billion a year*. Put another way, illegal immigration costs each Arizonan almost $700 a year—a hidden tax that subsidizes illegal aliens and those who hire them.

For most illegal aliens, Arizona is just a big transportation hub from which they travel to other parts of the country, and it is not unusual for immigration agents to find drop houses with over a hundred illegal aliens waiting for transport. We are routinely treated to headlines like these:

- "160 illegals caught in upscale Valley home"
- "Scottsdale home yields 71 illegal immigrants"
- "Another drop house found"

When I was first elected to Congress, I was pulled aside many times by concerned flight crews and flight attendants at Sky Harbor International Airport in Phoenix. They told me, "Congressman, please do something. Every night we are taking planes full of illegal aliens back east on red-eye flights. Where is the Border Patrol?" The real question is: where are the politicians?

I'll tell you where they are: they're AWOL.

Our Border Patrol is doing its job against incredible odds, but our immigration laws and a lack of resources work against it in sometimes shockingly stupid ways. Illegal aliens have learned to work the system. For example, OTMs cross into the United States from Mexico and immediately surrender to Border Patrol agents. Why? Simple. Since they are not Mexican citizens, OTMs cannot immediately be released back into Mexico, but must be deported to their home country, which can take months to arrange. According to Michael Chertoff, secretary of the Department of Homeland Security, "Today, a non-Mexican illegal immigrant caught trying to enter the United States across the southwest border has an 80 percent chance of being released immediately because we lack the holding facilities."[3]

Before being released, the illegals are given a court summons, better known as a "notice to appear," which allows them to legally remain in the U.S. pending an immigration hearing. The Border Patrol more accurately calls them "notices to disappear," since some 98 percent never show up for their hearing. This dodge is particularly popular with Brazilians, who don't need a visa to travel to Mexico.

According to a Copley News Service story,

[The OTMs'] quick and well-rehearsed surrender was part of a growing trend that is demoralizing the Border Patrol...."We used to chase them; now they're chasing us," Border Patrol agent Gus Balderas said.... The result is an unintended avenue of entry for a rapidly growing class of illegal immigrants from Central and South America who now see the Border Patrol more as the welcome wagon than a barrier.[4]

It is hard to believe we could be more welcoming than we have been. How many illegal aliens are in the U.S. today? It's impossible to say. The Congressional Research Service estimates that the illegal alien population increased from 1.9 million in 1988 to 10.3 million in

2004. In fact, according to a Pew Hispanic Center report, since the mid-1990s the number of illegal aliens coming to the U.S. has exceeded the number of new legal immigrants.[5]

A report published by Bear Stearns Asset Management concluded that the number of illegals may be as high as twenty million, or equal to the population of New York state. The Bear Stearns report also found:

- Since 1990, an average of 962,000 illegal aliens entered the country annually, although several reputable studies indicate that the rate could now be as high as three million.
- There are between twelve and fifteen million jobs in the U.S. currently held by illegal aliens, or about 8 percent of the workforce.
- Cell phones, the Internet, and low-cost travel have made it easier for illegal aliens to cross the border, find employment, and circumvent immigration laws.[6]

Not all of these illegals came across the Mexican border. The Department of Homeland Security estimates that 30 percent of all illegals are here because they've overstayed their visas, although the Government Accountability Office says that is probably somewhat understated. It is safe to say that three to four million illegals have overstayed their visas and that up to 150,000 join them every year.[7]

Rampant illegal immigration has a huge impact on crime and prison populations. It is an enormous burden on our health care, education, and welfare systems. It is changing our culture. But the biggest threat comes from the deadly combination of porous borders and weapons of mass destruction finding their way into the hands of terrorist groups.

Terrorists know all about our contradictory immigration policies. They have taken advantage of them before, and there is no reason to think they will not do so again. We ignore that fact at our own peril. In a post–September 11 world, we must not allow "political correctness" to cloud our thinking about the threat we face or to encourage terrorists to exploit that confusion. And we must ensure that Congress and the president act before the terrorists do.

THE TERRORIST THREAT

More than 500 million people annually cross U.S. borders at legal entry points, about 330 million of them noncitizens. Another 500,000 or more enter illegally without inspections across America's thousands of miles of land borders or remain in the country past the expiration of their permitted stay. The challenge for national security in an age of terrorism is to prevent the very few people who may pose overwhelming risks from entering or remaining in the United States undetected.

—The 9-11 Commission Report

In the summer of 2004, I took a helicopter tour of the Arizona-Mexico border. We flew over a rugged desert terrain of small mountains and valleys. A Border Patrol agent told me that most illegal aliens avoid the higher elevations, stick to known trails between the mountains, and travel in large groups.

But what stayed with me most was something else the agent said: that a determined and properly equipped enemy with military training—especially Islamic terrorists trained in the mountains of Afghanistan and Pakistan—would have no problem striking out over those mountains and sneaking into the country.

In testimony in February 2005 before the Senate Intelligence Committee, CIA director Porter Goss, Deputy Secretary of Homeland Security Admiral James Loy, and FBI director Robert Mueller offered a chilling assessment of the threats posed by al Qaeda against the American homeland. America's highest-ranking intelligence officials all agreed that terrorist organizations remain committed to obtaining and using weapons of mass destruction against the United States, with Goss stating, "It may only be a matter of time before al Qaeda or another group attempts to use chemical, biological, radiological, and nuclear weapons."[8]

Some time ago a captured terrorist related al Qaeda's plans to smuggle a nuclear bomb into Mexico and then across the border to the U.S. Admiral Loy testified:

> Recent information from ongoing investigations, detentions, and emerging threat streams strongly suggests that al Qaeda has considered using the southwest border to infiltrate the United States. Several al Qaeda leaders believe operatives can pay their way into the country through Mexico and also believe illegal entry is more advantageous than legal entry for operational security reasons. However, there is currently no *conclusive* [emphasis added] evidence that indicates al Qaeda operatives have made successful penetrations into the United States via this method.[9]

But what would conclusive evidence look like? Another September 11? A mushroom cloud? Some of the September 11 terrorists were in America for more than a year before they struck. They rented apartments, got driver's licenses, took flying lessons, and traveled freely. Several even had contact with law enforcement authorities. How do we know another such terrorist team is not here already? Again, the headlines say it all:

- "Syrians caught; in U.S. illegally"[10]
- "Mesa man accused of smuggling Iranians"[11]
- "Zarqawi Planning U.S. Hit? Intelligence officials say operatives may infiltrate via Central America to strike at soft targets on American soil"[12]
- "U.S. Calls Entry Point in San Diego a Possible Security Risk"[13]

In 2004 Border Patrol agents arrested more than 650 suspected terrorists from countries of "national security interest" trying to cross our southern border.[14] Remember, it is safe to assume that *at least* three illegals make it across the border for every one who is caught. As you do the math, keep in mind that it takes only a handful of committed terrorists to strike a devastating blow. It took only nineteen on September

11. It becomes even more unnerving when you pick up the newspaper and see headlines like this: "Border agent said to also be smuggler."[15]

That's right. A Border Patrol agent in San Diego was charged with conspiring to smuggle illegal aliens across the border. But the story took an even odder twist when it was discovered that the Border Patrol agent was himself an *illegal alien* who had used a fake birth certificate to get the job.

Sadly, these types of stories are getting to be more common. In another disturbing case, immigration enforcement officials arrested three illegal aliens, two Indonesians and a Senegalese, working as language instructors at the Army's Special Operations Command Center at Fort Bragg. These illegals also used false documents to get their jobs.

And let's not forget our Canadian border. As Admiral Loy stated:

In addition to the problems posed by the southwestern border, the long United States-Canada border, often rugged and remote, includes a variety of terrain and waterways, some suitable for illicit border crossings. A host of unofficial border crossings can be utilized when employing the services of alien smugglers, especially those winding through mountain ranges and across the vast western prairie.[16]

Canada—with which we share an almost 4,000-mile-long border patrolled by only about 1,000 Border Patrol agents—poses particular problems because it has been a refuge for terrorists. In his book *Cold Terror: How Canada Nurtures and Exports Terrorism to the World*, Stewart Bell writes that "Canada has become a source country of international terrorism," providing "money, propaganda, weapons, and foot soldiers to the globe's deadliest religious, ethnic, and political extremist movements." He says Canada has tried to "smother terrorism with kindness," something he calls a "typically Canadian approach." He laments that Canada's "most valuable contributions to the war on terrorism may well be its terrorists."[17]

We all remember the case of the alert Border Patrol agent who caught Ahmed Ressam trying to cross from Canada into Washington

State in a car packed with explosives. Ressam's plan was to blow up Los Angeles International Airport during the millennium celebrations. Canadian intelligence had apparently known about his terrorist links for years, yet did nothing to stop him.

Then there is the case of Fateh Kamel, who was jailed in France for terrorist-related crimes, including conspiring to blow up Paris Metro stations. After he was released he returned to Canada, where, according to the *National Post*, the Royal Canadian Mounted Police "was not even at the airport to greet him. As far as they're concerned, he is an ex-convict who has done his time and has committed no crimes in Canada."[18]

Even more recent, after the breaking up of a terrorist cell of an Islamist militant group, the Canadians allowed the al Qaeda–trained ringleader to freely leave Canada. Since Canadian law does not make it a crime to belong to a terrorist group, it is likely Canadian authorities felt they could not arrest or convict the terrorist. So instead they merely confronted him, prompting his voluntary departure.

Even in the wake of September 11, many of Canada's laws make it a safe haven for terrorists. David Harris, former chief of strategic planning for Canada's counterpart to the CIA, claims that more than fifty terrorist organizations have a presence in Canada. He says, "Canada has essentially said, if you put your foot in Canada and you declare yourself a (Geneva Convention) refugee, then by and large you are. All of that has implications; it means that we're quite susceptible to penetration."[19]

To be fair, there has been limited progress in Canada. But there are still too many "ex" terrorists north of the border.

TERRORISTS ON VISAS

Terrorists aren't limited to sneaking across our porous borders; they can, like many of the September 11 hijackers, enter on visas. What makes it all possible is document fraud. According to the 9-11 Commission, "for terrorists, travel documents are as important as weapons."[20] Indeed, document fraud has become big business—and sometimes government employees are involved.

A 2004 sting operation in Arizona by federal authorities resulted in the arrest of twenty-six state workers who were charged with illegally issuing phony driver's licenses and other identity documents to human smugglers, illegal immigrants, and drug dealers. Arizona Department of Motor Vehicles employees were charging $600 to $3,500 for each document.

More recently, a sting operation in Virginia led to the arrest of a Department of Motor Vehicles official, his wife, and another man for selling valid driver's licenses for as much as $3,500 (apparently the going rate!) to illegal immigrants. The Commonwealth is very sensitive about its driver's licenses, after seven of the September 11 terrorists were found to have had valid Virginia driver's licenses and state ID cards. (According to the 9-11 Commission, all but one acquired some form of U.S. identification document, some by fraud.) Virginia now requires applicants to provide documentation that they either are U.S. citizens or are in the country legally.

Federal authorities also uncovered a crime syndicate specializing in the distribution of millions of phony documents to illegal aliens nationwide (three million to the Los Angeles area alone), including high-quality Social Security cards, resident alien cards, driver's licenses, birth certificates, marriage licenses, work authorization documents, vehicle insurance cards, temporary vehicle registration documents, and utility bills from both Mexico and the U.S. It was so sophisticated that syndicate leaders would charge franchise fees for smaller cells to operate in the U.S.

What does the operational imperative to obtain documents mean in practice? Former 9-11 Commission counsel Janice Kephart studied ninety-four foreign-born terrorists who operated in the U.S. Here is what she found:

- About two-thirds committed immigration fraud prior to taking part in terrorist activity.
- In at least thirteen instances, terrorists overstayed their temporary visas.
- Fraud was used not only to gain entry into the United States, but also to remain in the country. Seven terrorists were indicted for acquiring or using various forms of fake

identification, including driver's licenses, birth certificates, Social Security cards, and immigration arrival records.

- Once in the United States, twenty-three terrorists became legal permanent residents, often by marrying Americans. There were at least nine sham marriages.[21]

Congress and the president have made important reforms since September 11 to address many of these issues. However, there are still too many gaps in the system. The Department of Homeland Security has now instituted a plan to track visitors entering and leaving the country. Called US-VISIT, the program requires that U.S. consulates obtain an index fingerprint before issuing a visa. The fingerprint is matched against a database to ensure the applicant is not a known criminal or terrorist. In the United States, immigration authorities check that the visa fingerprint matches the visa holder. US-VISIT is a good program that has already successfully prevented criminals and terrorists from entering the United States. Unfortunately, because the program exempts those coming from Mexico or Canada, it applies to only about 15 to 20 percent of visitors.

That's bad enough, but the really big question is this: What will happen when US-VISIT starts identifying large numbers of visitors who have overstayed their visas? Will the government take action to track them down and deport them? Or will they simply become another illegal alien statistic? According to a report by the Department of Homeland Security's inspector general, it is likely to be the latter.

The inspector general found that "deficiencies in the apprehension and removal process result in a minimal impact in reducing the number of overstays in the United States." Out of 301,046 leads received in 2004, just 4,164 were pursued, resulting in 671 apprehensions. Even then, the inspector general says, "very few" of those will be deported unless they also have a criminal record or are detained.[22]

Another problem is the Visa Waiver Program (VWP), which allows citizens of twenty-seven friendly countries to travel to the United States without a visa. The London bus and subway bombers would have all qualified for this program. Government officials say that with tamper-proof passports (now required) we will be able to verify that the holders are who they say they are. But even then, without the scrutiny that goes with getting a visa, VWP could be an easy route into the country for Islamist terrorists from places like Germany, France, Spain, and Great Britain.

The *Wall Street Journal* once scolded that lawmakers need "to distinguish between immigrants who bus tables and those who hijack airplanes,"[23] without giving any practical advice on how to make such a distinction. Here's the distinction I make: if the busboy is illegal, he should be deported. The hijacker should be executed.

Many who share the *Journal's* point of view claim that the solution is a guest-worker program that would legalize millions of workers now in the country illegally. One Border Patrol agent, Lee Morgan, a decorated Vietnam veteran, sums up the national security argument for such a program in a very personal way: "What if another 9/11 happened and I'm responsible? What if the bastards come across here in Arizona and I don't catch them because I'm so busy chasing a busboy or a gardener that I don't have time to do my job—my real job— catching terrorists? I don't know how I'll live with myself."[24]

I can assure Morgan that if terrorists cross into Arizona from Mexico and perpetrate another September 11, it will not be his fault—it will be the fault of our elected leaders for not doing what we know needs to be done. The Border Patrol agents confronting this enormous problem are truly national heroes. But they are overworked, outmanned, and up against an impossible task. Testifying before Congress, former Immigration and Naturalization Service agent William D. West tells it like it is:

> Border intercepts of terrorists are rare exceptions and not the rule. Cases identifying such suspects generally result from multi-agency counter-terrorism investigative efforts conducted within the interior of the U.S. well after these suspects have entered. The case of Mahmoud Youssef Kourani, an alleged Lebanese Hezbollah operative indicted in Detroit last year for terrorism support charges, who was

found to have been smuggled across the U.S. Mexico border, is a recent example.[25]

Given its current resources, the Border Patrol can't be blamed for failing to find Kourani out of the million-plus illegals that come across the border every year from Mexico. And as we will see later, any guest-worker program would only make the Border Patrol's job harder. We need to dramatically increase the size of the Border Patrol and give it the resources necessary to do the job. Additionally, maybe it's time to think about what even I believed unthinkable just a few years ago—putting troops on the border until we can get the situation under control.

MILITARY READINESS AND PRIVATE PROPERTY

Leo Banks is a writer based in Tucson, Arizona, who captures the reality of life for Americans living along the Arizona-Mexico border:

> [M]ost are decent folks caught up in the daily invasion of illegals who tramp across their land. Ranchers in hard-hit areas spend the first hours of every day repairing damage done the night before. They find fences knocked down and water spigots left on, draining thousands of precious gallons. And then there's the trash: pill bottles, syringes, used needles, and pile after pile of human feces.... One rancher told me about illegals who rustled one of her newborn calves. The intruders beat the twelve-hour-old animal to death with a fence post, then barbecued it on the spot.[26]

I have been to the border many times and I can tell you that Banks's description is spot on. The border is an ecological nightmare, and the costs of its repair are largely being borne not by the government, but by citizens—taxpayers who not only pay Uncle Sam every April 15, but who also foot the bill for illegal aliens from all over the world. Indeed, I've been told that repairing the property damage caused by illegal immigration can cost individual ranchers $50,000 or more a year.

At the Tohono O'odham Indian Reservation in southern Arizona, along the Mexican border, tribal leaders estimate that illegal aliens traversing their land leave behind six tons of trash *every day*.[27] At the nearby Marine Corps Air Station in Yuma, which I have visited on several occasions, they tell me that environmental damage caused by illegal aliens threatens the habitat of two protected species, the flat-tailed horned lizard and the Sonoran pronghorn sheep.

But the danger isn't just to property and animals. Our citizens are also threatened. The *Fort Worth Star-Telegraph* reported on south Texas rancher Kerry Morales:

> She says illegal immigrants move daily through her eighty acres outside Hebbronville, about fifty-four miles from the U.S.-Mexico border. They've cut down her fences, stolen her pickup, and even broken into her home—once rampaging into the bedroom and nearly strangling her, sparing her life only after she grabbed a gun. "Maybe twenty years ago the illegals were innocent, hardworking people," she said. "Not anymore. Now, they're extremely dangerous. They mean violence."[28]

I hear similar stories every time I visit the border. People will not let their children play in the yard unless they are with them and have armed themselves. Their dogs are routinely poisoned by illegals, who don't want them barking and alerting homeowners. Certain roads are too dangerous to drive on after dark. According to Banks, "If you're not careful they'll come around a bend at 100 mph and run you into a ditch or worse."

No one is immune. Illegal aliens broke into the home of Arizona congressman Jim Kolbe, ironically a sponsor of major guest-worker legislation, and made themselves right at home. They ignored valuables, but "showered, prepared a meal in the microwave, and helped themselves to a change of the congressman's clothes."[29]

Illegal aliens even brazenly cut across the borders of Fort Huachuca in Sierra Vista, Arizona, a sprawling U.S. Army facility that is home to the country's premier military intelligence school. In 2004,

3,086 illegal aliens were caught by Army personnel and turned over to the Border Patrol. Ironically, Fort Huachuca hosts units and military training commands from...the Department of Homeland Security!

The *Boston Globe* reported that "Marines preparing for combat in Iraq or Afghanistan have lost significant amounts of training time because undocumented immigrants from Mexico have constantly wandered onto a bombing test range in Arizona."[30] In 2003 the Marines intercepted more than 1,500 illegal aliens on the Barry M. Goldwater Range, which is used as a bombing test range by Marines at the nearby Marine Corps Air Station in Yuma. According to the Marines, illegal aliens traipsing across the range in 2004 caused the loss of more than 1,250 training hours, or more than fifty training days. This has a detrimental effect on the readiness of our troops and hurts our national security. Bill Richardson, a retired police officer, is outraged by what goes on, for good reason: "My son is a Marine and flies on a helicopter. His good buddy is a helicopter crew chief who's headed to Yuma, then Iraq. They belong to the Second Marine Air Wing. Will continued training interruptions cost them their lives?"[31]

When the Mexican government is asked for its help in stopping its citizens from overrunning our border, trespassing on our military installations, threatening our citizens, and destroying the private property of Americans, its officials demur. They claim they can do nothing because of a provision in their constitution that allows for freedom of movement (Article 11 begins, "Everyone has the right to enter and leave the Republic..."), even though under Mexican law it is illegal to leave the country except at designated crossing points.

So the "staging areas" in towns on the Mexican side of the border, from which thousands of illegal aliens of all nationalities make their way into the U.S., are left alone. (The use of the military term "staging areas" is appropriate since it is from these places that the illegal invasion of our country is launched. Paramilitary drug smugglers also use these areas as a base of operations.) In the immortal words of General Norman Schwarzkopf (used in a different context), the excuses constantly proffered by the Mexican government are "bovine scatology."

If the roles were reversed you can be sure that the Mexicans would be demanding restitution from us or would be taking us to the World Court. Maybe we should start demanding restitution from Mexico.

THE ECONOMIC THREAT

President George W. Bush's leadership in the War on Terror has been bold and inspiring. But when it comes to illegal immigration, he has been uncharacteristically and disturbingly vague and indecisive. Instead of the moral clarity we've come to expect, we get such politically correct buzz phrases as, "If an American employer is offering a job that American citizens are not willing to take, we ought to welcome into our country a person who will fill that job."

That's not a policy—it's a verbal tranquilizer meant to soothe the nerves of Americans who have had it with rampant lawbreaking on our border. As long as Americans have to compete with illegal aliens who will work for next to nothing, how can we know what jobs they won't take? There are many hard, dangerous, and dirty jobs that Americans would gladly take if they were paid a decent wage. Some open-borders conservatives—an oxymoron if ever there was one—call this competition with illegal aliens a "flexible labor market." In truth, it is a subsidy to businesses that exploit illegal labor.

There is no way to square free markets with illegal immigration. Illegal immigration actually distorts the free market, because it shields certain segments of the economy from the true cost of labor and prevents the "creative destruction" that is necessary to keep an economy competitive. "Creative destruction" is the term coined by economist Joseph Schumpeter to describe the process by which some jobs disappear as a result of innovation and eventually are replaced by better, more productive jobs. We witnessed this process throughout the 1980s, as low-skilled factory jobs were lost and replaced by high-tech jobs. By providing a bottomless supply of cheap labor, illegal immigration impedes that process of innovation and creative destruction.

Still, the temptation to hire illegals can be irresistible at times. For example, *Time* magazine reported this story:

The two Tyson managers who pleaded guilty contended that they had been forced to hire illegals because Tyson refused to pay wages that would let them attract American workers. One of those two managers was Truley Ponder, who worked at Tyson's processing plant in Shelbyville, Tennessee. In documents filed as part of Ponder's guilty plea, the U.S. Attorney's office noted, "Ponder would have preferred for the plant to hire local people, but this was not feasible in light of the low wages that Tyson paid, the low unemployment rate in the area from which the plant drew its workforce, and the general undesirability of poultry processing work when there were numerous other employment opportunities for unskilled and low-skilled employees.

"Ponder made numerous requests for pay increases in Shelbyville above and beyond what the company routinely allowed, but Tyson's corporate management in Springdale rejected his requests for wage increases for production workers. This refusal to pay wages sufficient to enable Tyson to compete for legal laborers, plus the limited workforce in the local area, dictated Ponder's need to bring workers in to meet Tyson's production demands." Needless to say, hiring illegals had benefits for Tyson. A government consultant estimated that the company saved millions of dollars in wages, benefits, and other costs.[32]

If employees work "off the books," the companies that hire them can save even more. One analysis done by *Newsday* found the cost in New York of hiring an off-the-books worker for $499 a week was just that, $499 a week. The cost for that same worker to an employer who obeys the law? Over $1,000 a week.[33] No wonder so many jobs are going to illegals in the underground economy.

Yet the same liberals who profess outrage at companies "outsourcing" American jobs to places like India couldn't care less when American workers lose their jobs to "insourced" illegal aliens. While Senator Ted Kennedy rails that "outsourcing enables profits to grow by sending American jobs abroad,"[34] he also claims that legalizing millions of illegal workers will protect "American workers' rights and wages, too."[35] Not so.

Harvard professor and immigration expert George Borjas estimates that between 1980 and 2000, immigration reduced the average annual earnings of American-born men by $1,700, or about 4 percent. American-born men without a high school education were hit even harder, with their wages reduced by 7.4 percent. Borjas also found that the "negative effect on native-born black and Hispanic workers is significantly larger than on whites because a much larger share of minorities are in direct competition with immigrants." Wages of black and Hispanic Americans who were born in this country were reduced by 4.5 and 5.0 percent respectively.[36] Where are Jesse Jackson and Al Sharpton when you need them?

The *Wall Street Journal* editors once wrote of the "human tide" overrunning our borders, "Mexico's loss is our gain."[37]

Whose gain exactly? No gain for workers, that's for sure. Borjas found that immigration actually widened the gap between rich and poor. While poor and less-educated Americans saw their wages drop, businesses and the wealthy were able to take advantage of a cheap, abundant supply of labor. As a result, according to Borjas, tens of billions of dollars were redistributed from low-income workers to rich folk.

One can only imagine the hue and cry if Congress proposed raising taxes on the poor by tens of billions of dollars so that the wealthier among us could enjoy more leisure. Yet that is the net result of rampant illegal immigration. It is a corrosive transfer of wealth from the poor to the rich. But far from being outraged by it, the open-borders crowd wants to codify it!

In a revealing opinion column in the *Arizona Republic*, liberal "community activist" Bill Searle spilled the beans, writing: "With no compassion, we recently voted for Prop 200 [a ballot initiative that denied public benefits to illegals], which coldly marks all 'illegals' as unwelcome in our midst—even as they willingly perform chores shunned by most of us, yet are essential to the privileged lifestyle to which we have become accustomed."[38]

There you have it: the real reason so many liberals and elites are willing to look the other way on illegal immigration. For them, it is not about the rule of law or national security or American workers—it is all about preserving their "privileged lifestyle."

So when the Chicago Council on Foreign Relations asked both "opinion leaders" and the public about guest-worker legislation, the results were predictable. A majority of the public (52 percent) said they opposed the plan, while 71 percent of the "opinion leaders" said they favored it—a gulf wider than the one named after Mexico.[39] Since these "opinion leaders" don't have to compete with illegal aliens for jobs and actually benefit from illegal labor, the results are not at all surprising. But where is the compassion for Americans on the lower rungs of the economic ladder?

The attitude of the open-borders crowd seems to be that as long as the lawns are groomed, the crops are picked (particularly the lettuce; more on that later), the dishes are washed, and the kids get their diapers changed, who cares?

PUTTING A PRICE TAG ON LAWLESSNESS

So how much does illegal immigration cost America? According to the Bear Stearns study, a lot. An estimated five million jobs have shifted to the underground economy, where workers collect wages on a cash basis and avoid income taxes. As a result of circumventing labor laws:

- "The social expenses of health care, retirement funding, education, and law enforcement are potentially accruing at $30 billion per year."
- "On the revenue side, the United States may be foregoing $35 billion a year in income tax collections because of the number of jobs that are now off the books."[40]

This does not include the other costs associated with illegal immigration, such as welfare payments for Americans displaced by illegal workers. Brian Gatton, a professor of history at Arizona State University, sums it up: "Economists concur that unskilled immigrants constitute a net cost to American citizens, using more in public services than they pay in taxes. Only two groups profit: the immigrants themselves and their employers, who pay a wage so low that other costs are passed on to taxpayers."[41]

Let's put these costs into perspective. As of this writing it is estimated that the federal government will spend a staggering $200 billion to rebuild in the wake of Hurricane Katrina. Yet that is about what three years of illegal immigration costs. If the government knew there would be a Katrina every three years and did nothing about it, wouldn't you say the government was being negligent? So why do we let it get away with ignoring illegal immigration and its costs?

Illegal immigration is a net economic loss for the United States, but is a big gain for countries like Mexico. Illegals send back (relatively) big paychecks and are one of Mexico's largest sources of foreign exchange. Mexico's Consejo Nacional de Población (National Public Council) estimates that Mexicans working in the United States contributed $17 billion to Mexico's economy in 2004 (up sharply from $13.4 billion in 2003), making them one of the top three sources of income in the country.[42] Illegal immigration is, as we'll see, Mexico's only growth industry.

SCHOOLS FOR ILLEGAL ALIENS

Since the Supreme Court's 1982 decision in *Plyler v. Doe*, school officials cannot ask students about their citizenship or refuse them a free public education. Since the Constitution grants Congress the exclusive power "to establish an uniform Rule of Naturalization" (Article I, Section 8), the Court's decision blatantly usurped congressional authority—yet another example of why we need strict constructionists on the Supreme Court.

As is often the case when the court legislates from the bench, the results have been disastrous. According to one study, the children of illegal aliens (a category that includes illegal alien children and U.S.-born children of illegal aliens) account for more than 15 percent of the K–12 student population in California. In Texas, Arizona, Illinois, and Nevada it is 10 to 15 percent. In eleven other states it is more than 5 percent.

The cost of educating these children runs to almost $29 billion a year—$12 billion for illegals and $17 billion for the U.S.-born children of illegals. In California alone the total cost is almost $8 billion. Take a look at the chart below of the ten states with the largest illegal immigration education costs.

WHAT ILLEGAL IMMIGRATION COSTS EDUCATION[43]
(IN MILLIONS OF DOLLARS)

STATE	ILLEGAL ALIEN STUDENTS	U.S.-BORN CHILDREN OF ILLEGAL ALIENS	TOTAL
California	$3,220.2	$4,508.3	$7,728.5
Texas	$1,645.4	$2,303.6	$3,949.0
New York	$1,306.3	$1,828.9	$3,135.2
Illinois	$834.0	$1,167.6	$2,001.6
New Jersey	$620.2	$868.2	$1,488.4
Florida	$518.0	$725.3	$1,243.3
Georgia	$396.7	$555.3	$952.0
North Carolina	$321.3	$449.8	$771.1
Arizona	$311.8	$436.5	$748.3
Colorado	$235.0	$329.1	$564.1

Naturally, any attempt at weeding out illegal students is met with howls of protest. In 2002, two brothers and their cousin were barred from attending a New Jersey public school when the superintendent discovered their parents were in the country illegally (the mothers were Canadian citizens here on expired tourist visas).[44] How do you think the parents reacted when they realized they had been discovered? Did they:

A. skedaddle back to Canada
B. beg the superintendent not to turn them in to federal authorities
C. contact their immigration attorney, who had the kids back in school the next week

If you guessed C, you're starting to get the hang of this! But why was the issue "when will these kids get back to school?" when it should have been "when will these families get back to Canada?" It's crazy.

But it gets even more bizarre. In Arizona, an investigation by state school superintendent Tom Horne found that Mexican residents were attending Arizona schools. They weren't just crossing the border and hopping the bus—the owner of a trailer park was renting empty lots to Mexican parents and offering utility bills to prove county residency. You can find similar situations all along the border, from Texas to California, so that is not even the weird part of the story. Before the investigation was completed, the *Arizona Republic* reported: "The controversy has put the small school district in Ajo...in turmoil. Already facing declining enrollment, the district stands to lose more than $425,000 in funding if the estimated eighty to eighty-five students who now catch the bus at the U.S.-Mexico border are culled from its rolls."[45]

Hard to believe, but since more students mean more dollars, school districts want to boost enrollment—even if it means hordes of illegal students. That's because the goal isn't ensuring that American kids get the best education possible; it is ensuring that the schools get the maximum funding possible. As the Ajo superintendent said at the prospect of a funding cut, "It would be a major blow. It would mean layoffs of staff."[46]

At a time when school budgets are under strain nationwide, it makes no sense to take on the burden of educating citizens of other countries to the detriment of our own students. And there can be no doubt that those most hurt by the influx of illegal students are American minority children already most at risk of failing school—many of them Hispanic.

Since the vast majority of these illegal students are Mexican citizens, this rip-off amounts to a huge subsidy to the Mexican government that it neither appreciates nor deserves. In fact, the billions we spend to educate Mexican children in our public schools dwarfs the $71 million in foreign aid we're sending to Mexico this year. It is another cost of illegal immigration that could be avoided by getting serious about enforcing our laws and securing our borders.

Professor Victor Davis Hanson notes that illegal immigration affects education in another way: it saps resources that could be used for other, better purposes. In California, he writes, "the question of concern for the underprivileged seems not always to extend to our own citizens. California, for example, has over 14,000 illegal aliens incarcerated in its prisons, costing yearly more than twenty times the annual budget of the underfunded new University of California at Merced—a college located where it could best serve underrepresented poor and minorities."[47]

Liberals always love to use that rhetorical tactic whenever the debate is over military spending or tax cuts. "Instead of tax cuts for the rich, we should be helping the poor!" Yet when the choice is between illegal aliens and America's poor, the liberals side with the illegals—another wonderful example of liberal compassion.

A PRESCRIPTION FOR DISASTER

You might be surprised to know that not only do we bear the costs of educating the children of illegal aliens, but our hospitals, by order of the federal government, have to provide illegals with free universal health care. Under the Emergency Medical Treatment and Active Labor Act, illegal aliens cannot be turned away for "emergency" medical treatment. As you probably guessed, these days nearly everything is considered "emergency" care, from a splinter to a drug overdose, and woe be unto the physician that turns away a patient on "non-emergency" grounds. The trial lawyers and immigrants' rights groups will be waiting in line to sue.

Of course, the same rules don't apply if you are an American citizen, as this report from FOX News makes clear:

> "We're citizens here. Why should somebody from another country that's here illegally get anything that we can't get? I mean that's dumb, that's not right," said Don Schenck, whose son is mentally disabled. Though the Schencks are uninsured, and considered poor by county standards, his father had to find a way to pay for Bill's care while thousands of others, in the country illegally, get it for free. "It makes you feel pretty bad when you're born in that country and you're handicapped and you've got a learning disability and you can't get medical," Schenck said.[48]

Illegal aliens know they can't be turned away for care, so they tend to use emergency rooms like a regular doctor's office. Meanwhile, the Border Patrol permits Mexican ambulance drivers to bring indigent patients to U.S. border hospitals under "compassionate entry."

Jim Dickson, the CEO of Copper Queen Community Hospital in the border town of Bisbee, Arizona, told *Time* magazine that his hospital has become "the trauma center for that stretch of northern Mexico" and that half of the free care his hospital gives goes to patients brought across the border. This has led to calls for using your tax dollars to build new clinics...not for Americans living along the border, but *in Mexico!*[49]

Some illegal aliens come here just for one expensive medical procedure or another. According to Ray Borane, mayor of Douglas, Arizona: "The city of Douglas is the major crossing point for illegals... and there have been some people who have come over here specifically to get dialysis or complicated eye surgery. They've established illegal residency in this country in order to thrive off the health care system."[50]

But that's not all. Children of illegal aliens born in the United States are American citizens and are thus entitled to welfare benefits, including Medicaid and Supplemental Security Income (SSI) disability payments. Madeleine Cosman, writing in the *Journal of American Physicians and Surgeons*, shows how this taxpayer rip-off has grown: "Immigrants on SSI, including legal aliens, refugees, and illegals with fraudulent Social Security cards, numbered a mere 127,900 aliens (3.3 percent of recipients) in 1982. By 1992 the numbers expanded to 601,430 entitled (10.9 percent of recipients). In 2003, this figure was several million (about 25 percent of recipients)."[51]

When you add it all up, the costs are astronomical. According to the Federation for American Immigration Reform, in 2004 the cost of unreimbursed medical care was about $1.4 billion in California, about $850 million in Texas, and about $400 million in Arizona.[52]

Although federal law demands that physicians and hospitals provide the care, the government is under no obligation to pay for any of it and goes to great lengths to avoid it. Again, according to *Time* magazine:

The Border Patrol officers—on orders from Washington—have refused to take [injured illegals] onto the hospital property after taking them into custody. Instead, the officers have called an ambulance for the injured. If the officers were to arrive at the hospital to make their drop-off, then the Border Patrol (make that the U.S. government) would be responsible for paying the medical bill. And that's something the federal government (make that Congress) will not do.[53]

This outrageous unfunded mandate has to stop. The government won't fulfill its obligation to control the border and it insists that illegals must be given free medical treatment—it should pay for it. In return, hospitals should be required to obtain citizenship information on their patients. The Medicare prescription drug plan enacted in 2003 did provide for modest payments to hospitals that treat illegal aliens, but these payments are only a fraction of what's needed. It also required that medical workers should "make a good faith effort to obtain citizenship information." Good faith isn't good enough.

In 2004, some of us in Congress tried to do something about this loophole. My Republican colleague Dana Rohrabacher of California offered an amendment to require hospitals to collect from all patients five pieces of information that would be submitted to the Department of Homeland Security: proof of citizenship, immigration status, address, current or former employer, and a biometric identifier such as a photograph or fingerprint.

In a post–September 11 world, this only makes sense. Yet even though hospitals collect vast amounts of information from patients already, this amendment was seen as "undermining the relationship of trust between health care providers and their patients." As ultra-liberal congresswoman Sheila Jackson Lee put it, "The effect of this amendment would be to require physicians and other health care providers to become part-time Border Patrol agents."[54]

Actually, when you see how the open-borders crowd strenuously objects to any enforcement of our immigration laws, it becomes clear that they don't even want Border Patrol agents to act like Border Patrol agents.

Incredibly, the House bought their nonsensical arguments and the proposal was rejected 331–88, an ominous sign of how difficult it will be to enact immigration reform centered on enforcement.

Far from being outraged by the situation, many on the Left insist that illegal aliens aren't getting enough free health care. A recent study published by the far-left *American Journal of Public Health* (AJHP) claims that immigrants actually use less than half the health care services provided to native-born Americans. According to the authors, "Our study refutes the assumption that immigrants represent a disproportionate financial burden on the U.S. health care system."[55]

Really? Someone needs to notify Los Angeles, where seven emergency rooms and sixteen clinics closed down in 2004 alone. They can tell the same to administrators at hospitals in Arizona and Texas that are sinking under the weight of providing free medical care to illegal immigrants. (Jim Dickson says his hospital in Bisbee will probably have to shut down in three years.)

Far more telling than anything in the AJHP study is that *illegal* aliens make up anywhere from 3 to 7 percent of the population, but are 15 percent of the uninsured, maybe more. Who pays the medical bills for these freeloaders? Taxpayers and charities do.

Furthermore, what about Medicaid and other health-related welfare payments given to America-born children of illegal aliens? While the direct beneficiary of such payments is a U.S. citizen, the illegal alien parents receive a substantial indirect benefit. Steve Camarota of the Center for Immigration Studies estimates Medicaid payments for such "anchor babies" cost the federal government—that means you— $2.5 billion in 2002.[56]

And it gets worse. Illegal immigration is not just bad for America's health care system—it may be literally bad for your health. This headline above a story in the *Palm Beach Post* says it all: "Perilous Infectious Diseases Up in County."[57]

They could have written "Country."

The increase is largely due to the huge influx of immigrants, both legal and illegal. As Madeleine Cosman writes, "Many illegal aliens harbor fatal diseases that American medicine fought and vanquished long ago, such as drug-resistant tuberculosis."[58]

Since illegal aliens are not screened for diseases, they can walk in with whatever disease seems to be the flavor of the day—drug-resistant tuberculosis (which can cost up to $1 million to treat), Chagas, acute hepatitis B, chronic hepatitis C, and sexually transmitted diseases.

Luckily, the number of immigrants with these dangerous diseases is small...at least for now. But health professionals worry that America will begin to reflect what is happening in the rest of the world, where many of these diseases, particularly tuberculosis, are reaching alarming proportions.

Someone petitioning to get into the country legally with any of these diseases would be denied entry. Yet an illegal alien with any of them who shows up at the hospital must be treated and released, no questions asked. And with many experts predicting that it is only a matter of time until we face a worldwide avian flu pandemic, securing our borders takes on an even greater urgency.

Health care is like every other facet of illegal immigration—the illegal alien gets the benefit, the American people get the bill. It's enough to make you sick...perhaps even terminal.

CHAPTER TWO

CRIME AND ILLEGAL IMMIGRATION

"We're seeing an alarming number of incidents involving the same type of violence that's become all too common in Mexico, right here in Dallas. We're seeing execution-style murders, burned bodies, and outright mayhem."[1]

—A former Dallas narcotics officer
to the *Dallas Morning News*

FOR MANY ILLEGAL IMMIGRATION apologists, a major reason to reform our immigration laws is the hundreds of illegal aliens who die each year trying to cross the border. In an editorial called "Never Acceptable," the *Arizona Republic* rightfully laments:

In each of the past two years the bodies of more than 200 people were found in the deserts along Arizona's border with Mexico.... They died because this country's hypocritical immigration policy enhances border security while ignoring the availability of jobs.... Solutions? There are proposals in Congress for a guest-worker program, but they have made little progress.[2]

In the same vein, when Arizona senator John McCain introduced his guest worker/amnesty bill on the floor of the Senate, he began with "some startling statistics that demonstrate the critical need for immigration reform." His first statistic was that 300 people had died trying to cross the border in 2004.[3]

The Reverend Robin Hoover, founder of Humane Borders, a group that puts water in the desert for illegal border crossers, flatly states,

"[Migrant] deaths are going to continue to be the single strongest measure of why we have to reform our laws."[4]

These deaths are as tragic as they are unnecessary. They do not, however, demonstrate why we have to reform our immigration laws; they demonstrate why we have to *enforce* our immigration laws. If our border with Mexico were sealed, as it should be, no illegal border crossers would be dying in the desert.

If it is reform the apologists seek, they need look no further than Mexico's economic and political systems, which conspire to make so many so desperate that they will risk their lives to leave. Yet the "root causes" crowd seems completely uninterested in what drives people to such desperation. They would rather blame our immigration policies, as if these deaths were somehow our fault. By turning a blind (encouraging) eye to illegal entry into the United States, the Mexican government is as complicit in the deaths of these people as the unscrupulous "coyotes"—the smugglers of illegal aliens who prey on their hopes and abandon them to a fate they do not deserve.

ILLEGAL ALIEN CRIME SPREE

The human toll of illegal immigration is not confined to the desert. There is another tragedy that takes place well away from the border, one we don't hear enough about, and one we don't do enough about. I am referring to those Americans murdered, raped, or assaulted by criminal illegal aliens each year. We are in the midst of what *Investor's Business Daily* has called a "mounting epidemic of preventable crime by illegal aliens."[5] Its human toll far exceeds the number of illegals who die along the border.

Although precise numbers are unavailable, based on what we do know, it is safe to assume that the number of Americans killed by illegal aliens since September 11 likely exceeds the number of American military deaths in Iraq and probably even the number of Americans killed on that terrible day.

Yet the silence from the politically correct elites about this crime wave is deafening. Where is the outrage? Where is the compassion for our fellow Americans who are the victims of these violent criminals?

Although our first priority must be to stop terrorists from breaching our borders, there are many vicious criminals who also see the U.S. as fertile ground for violence and whose impact on communities across the country is no less deadly. In fact, illegal aliens have committed many of the most heinous and sensational crimes in recent memory. Here are a few examples that I am sure you will remember:

- In 1999 police finally caught up with serial killer Angel Maturino Resendez, better known as the "Railroad Killer." Resendez is responsible for at least nine particularly brutal murders, several rapes, and other serious crimes. He had been in police custody several times, had been deported several times, and had even done jail time in Miami. Whenever he was thrown out, he was able to sneak back into the country with no problem.

- In April 2002 in Los Angeles, illegal alien Armando Garcia fatally shot Los Angeles County sheriff's deputy David March during a traffic stop. Garcia, a drug dealer, had been deported from the U.S. *four* times, once for carrying a Tec-9 machine pistol. At the time of the March shooting he was wanted on two counts of attempted murder—in Baldwin Park, California, no less (see Chapter Four). After killing Deputy March, Garcia fled to Mexico. Mexican authorities will not extradite the cop killer because under California law he could face the death penalty.

- On July 4, 2002, Hesham Mohamed Hadayet walked up to the El Al (an Israeli airline) ticket counter at Los Angeles International Airport and began shooting. He killed two and injured three others before he was shot dead by a security guard. A zealous Muslim with an intense hatred of Israel, Hadayet had been in the country illegally and was under consideration for deportation until his wife won a visa through the diversity lottery. This is a program that gives green cards to 55,000 lucky folks essentially drawn out of a hat—with no regard to whether they will contribute to this country.

- One of the triggermen in the 2002 D.C.-area sniper shootings, Lee Malvo, is an illegal alien from Jamaica. He came here as a stowaway, which should have resulted in his immediate deportation. But because he was considered low-risk—and because of lack of detention space—federal authorities let him go, pending his hearing. Within weeks he was on the road with sniper John Allen Muhammad.

- In Lake Worth, Florida, an illegal alien from the Bahamas, seventeen-year-old Milagro Cunningham, took an eight-year-old girl to a nearby landfill, where he proceeded to sexually assault her, choke her, and leave her for dead in a rock-filled trash bin. That the girl was found alive is a miracle. Cunningham had been arrested three times by the Palm Beach County sheriff's office, and not once was his immigration status investigated. He should never have been in the country, much less on the street.

- On Mother's Day in 2005, a nineteen-year-old illegal alien from Mexico gunned down Denver detective Donald Young. Raul Garcia-Gomez set an ambush for Young and his partner, John Bishop, after they refused to let him re-enter a baptismal party because he was unruly. Bishop, who was wearing a bulletproof vest, was only slightly wounded. In typical politically correct fashion, the *Rocky Mountain News* reported that Garcia-Gomez had "immigrated to Los Angeles from Durango, Mexico." Oddly enough, it was originally believed that Garcia-Gomez would not flee to Mexico because he had no family there. I know what you are thinking. No family in Mexico? How can that be? He's *from* Mexico! Where are they? The answer: in Los Angeles! According to his girlfriend, "All his family lives there [L.A.]. His mother, his father, uncles, cousins, grandparents." However, Garcia-Gomez did indeed flee to Mexico, where he "visit[ed] long-lost relatives, trying to get to know everyone." These long-lost relatives turned him in to Mexican authorities. Since Mexico won't extradite if there is the possibility of the death penalty or life without parole,

Denver district attorney Mitch Morrissey was forced to adjust the charges, and in July 2005 a formal extradition request was made. Even with the lesser charges the Denver D.A. estimates it will be a year before Garcia-Gomez is extradited.

I could go on...and on...and on. There is no end to these types of terrible crimes.

The nonpartisan Government Accountability Office (GAO) investigated just how big a problem criminal aliens are. The numbers are staggering.

In 2003 there were 46,000 criminal aliens in federal prison, at a cost of $1.3 billion dollars. Not all of these criminal aliens were illegal, but it is safe to assume that a large proportion of them were. That same year there were 74,000 illegal aliens in state prisons (at a cost of $880 million) and 147,000 illegal aliens in local jails.[6] The majority of all these criminals are citizens of Mexico.

In a follow-up study, the GAO examined the criminal history of these prisoners. It looked at 55,332 individual illegal aliens and found that

they were arrested at least a total of 459,614 times, averaging about eight arrests per illegal alien. Nearly all had more than one arrest. Thirty-eight percent (about 21,000) had between two and five arrests, 32 percent (about 18,000) had between six and ten arrests, and 26 percent (about 15,000) had eleven or more arrests.[7]

These are not just jaywalkers. GAO continues:

About 15 percent were property-related offenses such as burglary, larceny-theft, motor vehicle theft, and property damage. About 12 percent were for violent offenses such as murder, robbery, assault, and sex-related crimes.[8]

And those are just the ones in jail. According to Heather Mac Donald, perhaps the foremost expert on illegal aliens and crime, fully 95 percent of all outstanding warrants for homicide (1,200 to 1,500) in Los

Angeles are for illegal aliens, and up to two-thirds of all fugitive felony warrants (17,000) are for illegal aliens as well.[9]

Illegal immigrants are also directly responsible for the spike in gang violence, the only category of violent crime that is rising in the United States. In congressional testimony, Kris Kobach, professor of law at the University of Missouri–Kansas City, describes the threat these gangs pose:

> As one police officer told me recently, these gangs present a far more deadly threat than their predecessors. Compared to the dominant gangs of the early 1990s, which were composed primarily of U.S. citizens from inner-city areas, today's street gangs are composed overwhelmingly of illegal aliens and are more violent, more likely to kill, and more likely to operate within well-organized criminal networks that not only span the country, but span the continent.[10]

One such gang is the Mara Salvatrucha, or MS-13, which *Newsweek* called "the most dangerous gang in America."[11] MS-13, comprised of "street-tough Salvadorans," is a prime target of federal law enforcement. In fact, the FBI has created an MS-13 task force, in the first nationwide effort ever to go after a single street gang. MS-13 has more than 10,000 members and operates in thirty-three states and several Central American countries. Their weapon of choice is the machete. Like many criminal gangs, they are deeply involved in drug smuggling.

Another threat comes from a group called Los Zetas—specially trained Mexican drug cops who have turned criminal. The Zetas are particularly ruthless and have terrorized large parts of northern Mexico. They now operate in the United States and have been involved in home invasions, abductions, murders, extortion, and drug trafficking.

How brazen are the Zetas? At a briefing in my office, the FBI told me that one of its agents had heard the Zetas were out to get him. However, a Zetas commander called the agent *on his cell phone* to assure him that the Zetas did not have a bounty on him or any FBI agent. The Zetas commander then offered to kill the guy spreading the story!

Officials at the Organ Pipe Cactus National Monument, where drug smugglers murdered park ranger Kris Eggle in 2002, estimate that illegal aliens and drug smugglers outnumber hikers and campers. Smugglers also frequently use Native American and public lands to bring their drugs through Arizona. The Phoenix division of the Drug Enforcement Administration reports that law enforcement officials seize about 1,000 pounds of marijuana *a day* in the Tohono O'odham Nation. In April 2002, 9,000 pounds of marijuana were confiscated in a single seizure and an additional 6,000 pounds were captured days later.

Since 1994 Arizona has led the nation in per capita car thefts, thanks to illegal immigration. In 2002, 57,668 vehicles were stolen in Arizona, mostly by smugglers. Largely because of property theft by illegals, Arizona has the highest crime rate in the nation.[12]

The border itself is a veritable war zone. In the Tucson sector, Border Patrol agents are routinely assaulted, shot at, or rammed by smuggler vehicles. It is so bad that researchers studying desert wildlife on public lands along the border must be accompanied by park personnel. At the Organ Pipe Cactus National Monument researchers must have armed law enforcement with them in some areas closest to the border.[13]

Yet we barely hear a peep from the pro-illegal alien advocates about all the murder and mayhem caused by illegal aliens.

LETTING CRIMINALS RUN FREE

Why is it that some illegal aliens can be arrested an average of eight times and still be in the country? The most outrageous reason is "sanctuary."

You will find no better example of political correctness mixed with political cowardice than "sanctuary" policies. These policies forbid police officers from arresting criminals based only on their immigration status and prohibit local law enforcement from cooperating with federal immigration authorities.

The list of cities with sanctuary policies is quite long and includes some of the most liberal nationwide. It also shouldn't come as a surprise that some of these places boast the highest population of illegal aliens. According to the Congressional Research Service, these include: Anchorage and Fairbanks, Alaska; Chandler, Arizona; Fresno, Los Angeles, San Diego, San Francisco, Sonoma County, and San Jose, California; Durango and Denver, Colorado; Chicago, Evanston, and Cicero, Illinois; Cambridge and Orleans, Massachusetts; Baltimore and Takoma Park, Maryland; Ann Arbor and Detroit, Michigan; Minneapolis, Minnesota; Durham, North Carolina; Albuquerque, Rio Arriba County, and Santa Fe, New Mexico; Austin, El Cenizo, Houston, and Katy, Texas; Seattle, Washington; and Madison, Wisconsin. The entire states of Oregon and Maine are also sanctuaries.

These policies remain in force despite a 1996 federal law declaring that cities cannot prohibit their employees from cooperating with federal immigration authorities. New York City had a sanctuary policy that was repealed only after the brutal rape by five men of a forty-two-year-old mother of two in Queens. Four of the men were illegal immigrants and three had numerous prior arrests in New York for violent crimes. Yet the NYPD never contacted federal immigration authorities until after the rape. While one New York official assured Congress in February 2003 that "New York City has no 'sanctuary' policy for undocumented aliens,"[14] the city repealed it anyway just a few months later. Under pressure from supporters of illegal aliens, however, Mayor Michael Bloomberg instituted a similar "don't ask, don't tell" policy for the NYPD—that was "sanctuary" by other means.

Perhaps the most notorious sanctuary policy in the country belongs to Los Angeles. Issued in 1979 by the otherwise law-and-order Daryl Gates, the Orwellian-sounding "Special Order 40" prohibits the police from "initiating police action where the objective is to discover the alien status of a person." The only way the police can even ask about a suspect's alien status is to first arrest them for a crime.

Los Angeles attorney Carol Platt Liebau illustrates how this insane sanctuary policy makes the citizens of her hometown less safe:

As many as 30,000 illegal immigrants with criminal records are in L.A. County. The Los Angeles Police Department arrests about 2,500 criminally convicted deportees annually. But because of the sanctuary policy, they are arrested only after they have committed other crimes. If officers had the power to arrest previously deported criminals for immigration violations, they could prevent future crimes.[15]

L.A. chief of police William Bratton, who as police commissioner under Mayor Rudy Giuliani was one of the architects of New York City's amazing turnaround in crime, recognized the need to revise Special Order 40 to make it more flexible. He proposed new guidelines to give police new powers...but with several debilitating catches. Heather Mac Donald exposed the hoax:

> Special Order 40 has made Los Angeles into a free-fire zone for illegal gangbangers, who know that the police can't touch them for their immigration crimes. So what does the LAPD top brass propose to do? Confer due process rights on illegal *chollos* that your average Crips homie could only dream of possessing.
>
> Compare the fate of two gangbangers, one American, the other an illegal Mexican. Let's say a cop sees a member of the 42nd Street Gangster Crips hanging out with fellow Crips in a park that the gang controls. Congregating in the park is illegal under a local gang injunction. The cop can arrest all those Crips on the spot; he doesn't need to go before a judge to get an arrest warrant.
>
> Now imagine that that same cop sees an illegal alien member of the 18th Street gang hanging out on Cesar Chavez Blvd. The 18th Streeter has already been deported back to Mexico following conviction for murder. Upon deportation, he was forbidden from ever returning to the U.S. His mere presence in L.A. now is a federal felony punishable by twenty years in jail. Can the cop arrest him?
>
> Absolutely not—not under the old Special Order 40, nor under the proposed revision. According to the contemplated new rules, that cop first has to call his supervisor; that supervisor has to call federal immigration officials at ICE [Immigration and Customs Enforcement]; ICE officials have to go before a federal judge to get an arrest warrant; then, with warrant in hand, the cop may finally arrest the felonious 18th Streeter. Oops. He's gone.[16]

Of course, even these cosmetic changes have been greeted with howls of protest from the usual left-wing suspects, including the City of Los Angeles Human Relations Commission, the Mexican American Legal Defense Fund, the National Immigration Law Center, Casa Nicaragua, El Rescate, National Central American Roundtable, the Mexican American Bar Association, the American Civil Liberties Union (ACLU), and the LAPD Hispanic Community and Asian Pacific Islander Forums. Apparently they are more concerned with the "rights" of illegal aliens than the safety of our fellow citizens.

The ACLU speaks for all these groups when it claims that without sanctuary, "immigrants will become easy prey for criminals who know the victims will not report offenses to the police for fear of being deported."[17] In other words, the ACLU actually believes that sanctuary policies reduce crime! This is pure fiction.

Federal law enforcement authorities tell me privately that one of the reasons the human smugglers and gang members feel they can murder, rape, enslave, or steal each other's human cargo is that they know no one is going to report anything, sanctuary law or no. And yet mayors and local police chiefs remain wedded to the idea that they can win the trust of illegals. According to Phoenix mayor Phil Gordon:

> Our [police] officers depend on trust and communication at the neighborhood level to identify criminal activity and get the cooperation of victims and witnesses. If our officers essentially become INS agents, if racism allows one neighbor to report on another because they "look foreign," and if we blur the role between local and federal enforcement, we will jeopardize that trust.[18]

The problem is that the trust the mayor describes doesn't exist. The *New York Times* reveals the truth about the situation in Phoenix:

> Many illegal immigrants said they were reluctant even to call 911 when they needed help. A friend of Benito said they were afraid that the police would arrive with immigration agents. "That's why they

are still selling crack over there," he said, pointing to the house across from Benito's. "Nobody around here complains."[19]

To help convince illegal aliens to help law enforcement solve crimes, Congress passed a law in 2000 that would give those who assist in the investigation and conviction of serious crimes a special visa that would let them live and work legally in the United States. However, bureaucratic inertia has prevented even one such visa from being issued. As a result, nine illegals filed a lawsuit against the federal government, demanding visas for helping law enforcement.

The illegals' attorney complained, "As a result [of the federal government's inaction], thousands of violent crimes continue to go unreported because immigrants are reluctant to cooperate with police, fearing they will be deported."[20] What was that again about "trust"?

It is our own fault that illegal alien felons wander the streets of America's cities beyond the grasp of law enforcement. Under a rational system of law enforcement that puts public safety over political correctness, a gang member recognized as being in the country illegally would be picked up by local police and turned over to federal authorities for immediate deportation.

Under the ACLU's idea of law enforcement, we leave the gangbanger alone until he commits *another* crime, possibly murder. Only a liberal could believe that letting deportable felons roam the streets will reduce crime.

CATCH AND RELEASE: SAVE IT FOR THE FISH

It is a mystery why so many illegals fear detection and deportation when the chances of them actually being caught and deported are so remote. Even when local police actually do cooperate with federal immigration authorities, many times the feds drop the ball because of a lack of resources and other obstacles. As a result, there are about 465,000 illegals with pending deportation orders on the loose.

In testimony before a Senate subcommittee, deputy assistant attorney general Jonathan Cohn stated that the U.S. has had to release into the community numerous illegal aliens who are murderers, rapists, and child molesters. Why? Because after having served their sentences, criminal aliens—by ruling of the Supreme Court—can only be held in prison for six months pending deportation.[21] If the criminal alien's home country refuses to accept him within that time, the criminal is cut loose.

As bad as that is, the real problem is not the Supreme Court, but the fact that we are trying to enforce our immigration laws on the cheap. The Bureau of Immigration and Customs Enforcement (ICE), which enforces immigration laws in the interior of the country, has been shortchanged for years. It doesn't have enough beds or detention space to hold illegals for deportation. It doesn't have enough agents (only 2,900 or so for the entire country) and it doesn't have enough funding.

Heather Mac Donald points out that in the early 1990s just fifteen immigration agents were responsible for the deportation of approximately 85,000 aliens in New York City.[22]

As a result, ICE agents prioritize who they go after, and most of the time they focus on cases involving aggravated felons, smuggling, physical abuse, sexual crimes, firearms, or unaccompanied juveniles. Having to pick and choose can have disastrous consequences.

Rodrigo Cervantes Zavala is the accused killer of three people in Queen Creek, Arizona, in 2005. They were the grandparents and uncle of his two children by his estranged girlfriend. They died because they would not hand over the children to Cervantes, who then kidnapped them and took them to Mexico, where he was captured and now awaits extradition (as we've seen, extradition is a long shot). His is a case study in how the lack of resources fails the American people.

Cervantes was told almost ten years before the murders that he had to "voluntarily" leave the country, but he came back. In 2004, he was arrested on suspicion of felony burglary, but was released on his own recognizance. Immigration authorities were notified but did not respond in time to detain or deport him. Cervantes showed up for his trial, was convicted of felony burglary, and given a two-year probation. ICE was again notified, but since Cervantes was considered a low-risk illegal alien, he never fell into the hands of immigration authorities. A year later he was an alleged murderer.

How many more like Cervantes are out there? Can we afford to find out?

Most of the time, even a final deportation order is a futile gesture. Instead of immediately getting the boot, illegals will get a notice from ICE *asking* them to show up for deportation. For obvious reasons, these are known as "run letters." And run the recipients do. A February 2003 Justice Department report lists the percentages of aliens who have been so notified but never show up for deportation:

- 87 percent overall
- 94 percent from countries that sponsor terrorism
- 65 percent of criminals
- 97 percent of those denied asylum[23]

Manny Van Pelt, a spokesman for U.S. Immigration and Customs Enforcement, admitted the obvious to the *Los Angeles Times*: "The nation's immigration system is largely based on personal integrity. We have seen that the honor system does not work."[24] I'll say.

ICE is now testing in eight cities electronic bracelets and voice recognition systems that allow agents to keep track of illegal aliens pending deportation. Of course, even this is too much for the usual suspects. Anamaria Loya, executive director of La Raza Centro Legal in San Francisco, says, with a straight face, "It's treating them the way we in society treat criminals."[25] Hey, Anamaria, they *are* criminals!

ICE agents are so overworked that in many jurisdictions local police simply stop calling them because they know they will not get a response. Retired Mesa, Arizona, police officer Bill Richardson writes: "Cops up and down the chain of command continually tell me that federal authorities are nowhere to be found when they need help with illegal aliens. Unless it's a big case that'll get them good press, the feds just don't give a damn."[26]

Indeed, in my home state of Arizona, ICE has reached an understanding with local law enforcement. The locals won't call ICE unless a prosecutable crime has been committed (usually involving firearms, drugs, or a violent crime) or if there are at least thirty illegal aliens involved. In practice, this "understanding" means that if local police call ICE about a disabled van full of illegal immigrants, unless ICE agents show up within a half hour or so, the illegals are let go.

It is called "catch and release," and it has become so commonplace that sometimes illegals expect to be released and are surprised when they aren't. Between 1999 and 2001, several police departments in Orange County, California, began transporting illegal aliens arrested on minor offenses to the INS (Immigration and Naturalization Service, now CIS) checkpoint in San Clemente. One such incident is particularly revealing. Here is how the *Los Angeles Times* reported it:

> Anger boiled anew last week over an eighteen-year-old Anaheim woman who was taken into custody by police after a traffic stop for an expired registration. An INS agent determined that Marcella Duque was in the country illegally, and the native of Colombia now faces deportation.
>
> Outraged Latino activists have demanded that Anaheim break its INS ties.
>
> "I had heard that if you were stopped for driving without a license, the police would take your vehicle away but let you go," Duque said.
>
> "I was surprised that I was taken to jail and more surprised when they told me I was going to be deported."[27]

There is so much packed into those four paragraphs it is hard to know where to begin. There is the politically correct description of Duque as an "Anaheim woman" instead of an illegal alien. The "Latino activists," right on cue, brazenly demanding that one law enforcement agency not cooperate with another (they also, predictably, accused police of "racial profiling"). But it is the hapless Duque, "surprised" that law enforcement would actually enforce the law, who says so much about the state of our illegal immigration policy. Given the way we've failed to enforce our immigration laws, her surprise is understandable. Frankly, I'm surprised too.

IDENTITY POLITICS CAN BE
HAZARDOUS TO YOUR HEALTH

What is driving liberal big-city mayors to undermine our immigration laws? A little thing known as "identity politics."

Many cities have become inundated with immigrants, both legal and illegal, over the past two decades. With the increase in numbers has come an increase in political power, and many of these groups are not afraid to use it.

In September 2004 in Columbus, Ohio, a tragic fire swept through an apartment building, killing seven Mexican illegal aliens and three "anchor babies." Fire officials, who suspect arson, say members of the Hispanic community seem "uncomfortable about coming forward with information."[28]

In response, the West Side Fire Community Task Force was formed. It wants "911 operators to be prepared to handle Spanish-speaking callers and members of the Latino community trained to help when disasters strike."[29]

Sounds reasonable enough. But there's more. The task force also asked "that law enforcement officials protect crime victims and those who report crimes from the threat of deportation."[30] In other words, sanctuary.

Why would local politicians give in to that kind of blackmail? Most politicians are quite simply too cowardly to confront the reality of illegal immigration for fear of offending immigrant groups. An editorial in the *Chicago-Sun Times* shows how powerful a political force these groups can be. Writing about the prospect of legislation in the state of Illinois banning the use (as an acceptable form of ID) of the matrícula consular card issued by the Mexican government, the paper wrote:

If passed here, it would mean bad news for elected officials in Chicago, Hoffman Estates, Waukegan, Cicero, Melrose Park, Northlake, Round Lake, and Stone Park, who last year fell over themselves dancing to the music of Carlos M. Sada, Mexico's consul

general in Chicago. The standard format used by Mexican officials
to present their case includes showing up with a contingent of well-
rehearsed illegal aliens, which causes local officials to break into a
nervous sweat and quickly forget whose interests they were elected
to represent.[31]

Even in our nation's capital, immigration law is ignored. Washington, D.C., police chief Charles Ramsey, under pressure from the Latino
Lawyers Association, agreed in 2003 to "reiterate" a 1984 executive
order that prohibits D.C. police officers from asking people about
their immigration status during routine stops.[32]

Illegal alien interest groups can make even the bravest of politicians go weak in the knees. For instance, the rock-tough Rudy Giuliani
sued all the way up to the Supreme Court to defend New York City's
sanctuary policy against federal law. He lost.

The political correctness that typifies all facets of illegal immigration allows street gangs to act with extreme ruthlessness. Some in law
enforcement believe that alien gang members will sometimes pur-
posely kill their victims execution-style and then flee to Mexico,
secure in the knowledge that they will never be extradited for such a
capital crime. If that's true, political correctness actually encourages
first-degree murder.

Please don't confuse politicians and police chiefs with street cops,
who understand the connection between crime and illegal immigration and would like to use immigration violations as another way to
stop the bad guys. The politicians and police chiefs won't let them.

And it is not just city officials who feel the heat. Federal officials
feel it too. When a union representative went public with complaints
about how the Lee Malvo immigration case was handled, a Border
Patrol agent responded this way in an e-mail:

Your agenda, whatever it may be, is counterproductive to the thousands of (detention and removal) personnel who are doing their best
in spite of the limitations placed upon them by Congress, uncoopera-
tive foreign consulates, (non-governmental organizations), pro bono

attorneys, special interest groups, etc. Have you ever detained a non-criminal mother and her sixteen-year-old child for a lengthy period of time? Have you had to face the wrath of the above-mentioned groups?[33]

We know that these left-wing activist groups are nasty, ruthless, well organized...and wrong. Instead of kowtowing to them, it is time to fight them. It is a fight we can win.

Conservatives instinctively understand the nexus between illegal immigration and crime—liberals don't, or if they do, they don't care. In fact, some of them even get caught up in the whole illegal lifestyle, as happened in Phoenix.

In March 2004, U.S. immigration officials arrested Lizabeth Ramon de Harvey, a "Latina activist," as she attempted to smuggle two recently deported illegal aliens back into the country, a felony that carries a punishment of up to five years in jail and a fine of $250,000. De Harvey is no ordinary smuggler, however. At the time of her arrest she was the live-in girlfriend of Phoenix assistant police chief Silverio Ontiveros. She also served on the Phoenix Police Department's Hispanic Advisory Board.

De Harvey accepted a plea agreement of one-year probation offered by the U.S. Attorney's Office. The punishment did not even include community service. I was told her sentence is standard for first-time offenders. But given her position and the fact that she was unrepentant and remains as strident as ever (she even refused to resign from the advisory board and had to be thrown off), I believe such leniency sends the message to potential smugglers, illegal aliens, and the public that we aren't serious about enforcing our immigration laws, and I wrote Attorney General John Ashcroft saying so.

The Justice Department wrote me back defending its decision, saying: "Of necessity, the Arizona [U.S. Attorney's Office] has focused its resources on violent offenders, individuals who risk the lives of others, and smugglers of large numbers of aliens....By focusing on the most egregious violators of immigration law, we aim to deter a broad range of immigration violations."

It is understandable that the Justice Department wants to focus on violent offenders; such criminals need to be taken off the street. But claiming that focusing on "egregious violators" will "deter" other immigration violations is like saying focusing on bank robbers will deter shoplifters; it is backwards. The way to deter major crime, as we now know from experience, is by vigorously prosecuting *lesser* crimes.

CLEARING THE AIR

George Kelling and James Q. Wilson's "broken windows" theory is based on the observation that if a broken window in a neighborhood goes unrepaired, it is an indication the neighborhood has other, more serious problems as well. It also applies to crime. If the authorities let minor violations slide, this neglect rapidly escalates into an atmosphere of bigger, more prevalent crimes. In terms of policing, it means that by paying more attention to lesser infractions—such as graffiti, turnstile jumping, and, in a saner world, immigration violations—the police instill a respect for the law, which leads to a reduction in major crimes. New York City began tinkering with the theory in 1990 and in 1994 it was fully implemented by police commissioner William Bratton. The results were no less than spectacular, and New York became a livable city again.

On a national level, to paraphrase journalist Mark Steyn, the windows of our country are broken, and through them climb pretty much anyone who wants to be here.

If we want to get a grip on our illegal immigration problem, we need to adopt the "broken windows" theory of policing to immigration enforcement. Indeed, the 9-11 Commission staff report concluded, "The routine enforcement of laws, including those not specifically related to terrorism, can...raise obstacles for and in some cases have a deterrent effect on individuals intending to commit terrorist attacks."[34] As we know, police stopped several of the September 11 hijackers for traffic violations.

A good way to start undoing the damage would be enacting the Clear Law Enforcement for Criminal Alien Removal Act, or CLEAR Act, which would provide additional federal aid to local jurisdictions that allow their police departments to help enforce our nation's immigration laws. A May 2005 Zogby poll found that a huge 81 percent of Americans want local and state police to help federal authorities enforce laws against illegal immigration.

Still, the bill has bitter opponents who claim it would lead to "racial profiling" and "discrimination" and that "illegals won't report crimes if they perceive the police are part of immigration enforcement." (We've already seen what a crock that is!)

My hometown paper, the *Arizona Republic*, is typical. It says it "opposes the CLEAR bill in Congress that would authorize police to arrest undocumented immigrants crossing the border illegally. We believe this responsibility is best left to federal authorities."[35]

What? Police shouldn't enforce the law? How crazy is that? Besides, federal law *already* gives local police the authority to make arrests for immigration violations. And with only a handful of interior enforcement agents in the field, federal authorities simply don't have enough manpower. CLEAR is a force multiplier.

Thankfully, there are some in local politics and in local law enforcement who "get it." And unlike their liberal big-city counterparts, they do the right thing knowing the media and the liberal interest groups are going to go after them tooth and nail.

In New Ipswich, New Hampshire, police chief W. Garrett Chamberlain charged an illegal immigrant, Jose Mora Ramirez, with trespassing. Predictably, illegal immigrant activists went ballistic, but the chief told the *Washington Post*, "I'm just saying: 'Wait a minute. We're on heightened alert and it's post–9/11, and I'm going to let an illegal immigrant who I don't know from Adam just walk away?' That's ridiculous....I'm not going to worry about political correctness."[36]

The ACLU helped find a lawyer for Ramirez paid for by...the government of Mexico! The local ACLU spokesman parroted the party line, "The Mexican government was understandably worried that this could become the charge du jour across the country. They worry about vigilante police chiefs who will round up people based on the color of their skin."[37]

In the little town of Elsmere, Delaware, councilman John Jaremchuk proposed an ordinance to fine undocumented residents $100 if they are stopped by the police (after heavy pressure from the Democratic governor, it lost by a 5–2 vote). Jaremchuk said illegal immigration was draining town resources and declared, "The federal government apparently has no time to go after these individuals, so local government will step in."[38] Sounding like a broken record, Maria Matos, executive director of the Latin American Community Center of Wilmington, complained: "This is a racial profiling ordinance if I've ever seen one."[39] Racial profiling...click...racial profiling...click... racial profiling...click...How about recognizing that it's not about race, but about enforcing the law?

In California, Republican state senator Ray Haynes is working to establish a new California border police to enforce federal immigration law, including going after businesses that hire illegals. Haynes says the initiative would save California taxpayers at least $10 for every dollar it costs. Assembly Speaker Fabian Nunez responded, "I would hope that the days of anti-immigrant bashing are behind us. We ought to be celebrating our diversity."[40] Frankly, I don't see why illegal immigrants are necessary to celebrate our diversity. In fact, the invasion of illegal aliens predominantly from Mexico mocks our "melting pot" heritage and actually makes us *less diverse.*

Men like Senator Ray Haynes and the others who believe in defending our border understand better than any big-city liberal politician or police chief that illegal immigration is a national concern that requires the cooperation of law enforcement at every level. They deserve our gratitude.

IS IT WORTH IT?

At some point, the identity-group grievance-mongers and the politicians who kowtow to their intimidation tactics have to ask themselves: Is it worth it? Is what we gain from turning a blind eye to illegal immigration and its attendant crime worth the cost we pay?

The liberals, of course, say the answer is to grant amnesty to the illegal aliens, which they claim would free the Border Patrol and interior enforcement agents to go after the "real" bad guys. But how does anyone know for sure who the real bad guys are? Observing Millennium bomber Ahmed Ressam in court, investigative reporter Stewart Bell wrote, "He never looks more dangerous than a librarian, and that may be the scariest part of all."[41]

While the vast majority of illegal aliens come here to work, it only takes a handful of bad ones to cause mayhem and chaos on a grand scale. Since there is no way to distinguish with any certainty which illegal alien is a threat, we must not make any exceptions to our immigration laws or look the other way because of something as silly as a lack of bed space or a mayor who wants to score points with the ACLU and ethnic activists.

On this issue, the Justice Department takes my side:

> We also noted that the INS dedicated most of its effort toward removing criminal aliens. Although we do not question the need to remove criminal aliens, the result of INS's current approach is that little effort is directed at the large number of non-criminal absconders who may also pose a threat to the United States.[42]

The solution is obvious: Get serious about deporting those caught violating our immigration laws. Stop catch and release. Allow authorities to hold criminals indefinitely while they await deportation. Give enforcement personnel adequate resources. Get local police involved in enforcing immigration laws as a force multiplier. And adopt "broken windows" policing so that illegals expect to be deported if they are caught by police.

There is no doubt that this can be done while upholding our values as a nation of liberty and justice for all.

CHAPTER THREE

ASSIMILATION: OUT OF MANY...?

> *"We're Americans, with a capital 'A.' You know what that means? Do ya? That means that our forefathers were kicked out of every decent country in the world. We are the wretched refuse. We're underdogs! We're mutts!"*
>
> —John Winger, in *Stripes*

*T*HE STATUE OF LIBERTY is rightly one of America's most recognizable and uplifting monuments. A gift from France, it was originally designed to inspire the peoples of Europe to develop their own democratic societies. With the addition to its base years later of the Emma Lazarus poem "The New Colossus"—"Give me your tired, your poor, your huddled masses yearning to breathe free..."— the Statue of Liberty became synonymous with our immigrant heritage. At the rededication ceremony following its restoration, Ronald Reagan famously spoke these words:

You can go to France and can never become a Frenchman. You can go to Japan and never become Japanese, or Chinese, or German, or whatever. But anyone can come from anywhere and become an American.

Assimilation is the key to any successful immigration policy, and no country in the history of the world has succeeded in assimilating immigrants as well as the United States. Turning immigrants into Americans didn't happen by accident, but instead was the result of a comprehensive national effort. This assimilation process worked so well that the American Enterprise Institute's Ben Wattenberg came up with a new term to describe America, calling it the world's first "universal nation." Indeed, just because your ancestors came over on the *Mayflower* doesn't make you more American than the immigrant from India, the Philippines, Mexico, Mozambique, or elsewhere who took the oath of citizenship yesterday.

The ever-so-successful assimilation process that used to be called "Americanization" was a major movement in the early 1900s, with institutions at all levels of society and government doing their part. The public schools helped Americanize immigrant children. The YMCA offered English classes. The Catholic Church used its leverage to convince immigrants to leave the old ways behind and embrace American culture. The state of Connecticut even established a Department of Americanization. Large corporations taught their employees English and civics.[1]

Henry Ford, a leader in this movement, said, "These men of many nations must be taught American ways, the English language, and the right way to live." Talk like that today and our liberal elites will brand you a cultural imperialist, or worse. But if you ask me, Ford had a better idea.

Sadly, Americanization has given way to an insidious multiculturalism, the noxious idea that all cultures are equally valid and equally worthy. In the mid-1980s, the late Alistair Cooke, himself an immigrant, lamented the "general movement in the United States to unmelt the melting pot, to break down the goulash of the pot into its ethnic ingredients: to return, in short, to the immigrant compounds which Teddy Roosevelt was determined to fuse into one nation."[2]

So instead of Americanization, we offer bilingual education, racial and ethnic quotas, and education that focuses not on *American* heroes and culture, but on a potpourri of ethnic heroes and cultures. We print multilingual ballots and driver's license tests. Schools and hospitals have government-funded—make that *taxpayer*-funded—translators. Immigrants are encouraged to not just preserve their language and heritage, which they should, but to have their language and heritage compete with and replace our own. These efforts have only succeeded in isolating immigrants, linguistically and culturally.

As for Americans, we are supposed to mute whatever quintessentially American characteristics we possess for fear of appearing nationalistic or nativist. Indeed, we are told we should no longer even consider ourselves Americans: we are citizens of the world! Samuel Huntington illustrates the turnaround: "In the early 1900s, Ford was the corporate leader in promoting Americanization. In the 1990s, Ford quite explicitly defined itself as a multinational, not an American corporation."[3]

Henry Ford must be spinning tires in his grave!

WOULD YOU LIKE SOME ILLEGAL IMMIGRATION WITH THAT TOSSED SALAD?

There is no doubt that America is the most diverse nation in the history of mankind. Many like to say that our diversity is what makes America strong, but they have it backwards. Diversity is not the source of America's strength; it is the product of it. In most of the world diversity is the exception, not the rule. It is different here because America is different.

Yet the sad fact is that those on the Left simply do not believe America is in any way special—certainly not Ronald Reagan's "shining city on a hill." They don't see America as a melting pot, but as more of a "tossed salad"—a multicultural entity where racially and ethnically diverse peoples peacefully coexist, but never bond into a true unified community with a common purpose.

With each passing day America is becoming more divided by ethnicity, race, language, and income—a situation exacerbated by illegal immigration. We all had a good laugh when Al Gore mangled the translation of E pluribus unum. "Out of one, many," he goofed. But maybe he was just ahead of his time.

The Left doesn't want America to transform immigrants; it wants immigrants to transform America—culturally, economically, and especially politically. They believe immigration will benefit the Democrats, who have become the party of ethnic grievance. And what better way to speed up the process than to grant amnesty to the millions of illegal aliens in our country?

But many on the Right are to blame, too. Lots of conservatives think we can't do without the illegals' low-cost labor and assume that assimilating millions of them is easy. After all, they argue, the percentage of foreign-born people in the United States is lower today than it was in the high immigration years of the late nineteenth and early twentieth centuries.

Such optimism is unfounded because it ignores a fundamental difference between immigration then and now. Unlike those earlier periods of immigration, the current influx is comprised overwhelmingly of just one group—Mexicans. In 1920 the two largest groups of immigrants were Germans and Italians, who together totaled 24 percent of overall immigration.[4] Today, Mexico alone accounts for an unprecedented 30 percent of overall *legal* immigrants. Factor in millions of illegal immigrants, 60 to 70 percent of whom are Mexican, and the percentages explode. As a result, banks, phone companies, public utilities, businesses, and some local, state, and federal government offices offer to answer calls in English or Spanish, but not Korean, Hindi, French, or Russian.

Allowing one nationality to dominate immigration this way not only violates one of the bedrock principles of our immigration policy—diversity of admission—but also makes assimilation nearly impossible. Out of one, many. But out of two, what?

The answer may be a breakdown in social cohesion. Mark Steyn makes the point: "If there are three, four, or more cultures, you can all hold hands and sing 'We Are the World.' But if there are just two, that's generally more fractious. Bicultural societes are among the least stable in the world."[5]

I am concerned that we could be headed that way faster than anyone realizes.

THINK "AMERICA FIRST"

The longer the flood of illegal aliens from predominantly one country continues, the less incentive there will be for cultural assimilation.

And as Charles Krauthammer rightly argues, "If you don't assimilate the immigrants, then immigration becomes not an asset but a liability."[6] The evidence suggests that we are rapidly reaching that point—if we haven't arrived already.

As the British Broadcasting Corporation (BBC) reported in a May 30, 2005, radio documentary:

> The Latinization of California is nothing short of a revolution. California will become a predominantly Spanish-speaking state within the next few years. And, as the majority population, there is really no need, or incentive, for them to assimilate into mainstream American society as their predecessors have always done. Whether Latinos then decide to push for greater autonomy, to seek a political agenda of their own with closer ties to Mexico and Central America, is very much up for grabs.

These aren't the words of an anti–illegal immigrant fringe group, but the analysis of the widely respected and reliably left-wing BBC. If they get it, why do so many conservatives remain clueless?

A billboard promoting a Spanish-language TV newscast in Los Angeles showed the anchor team with the city in the background. Superimposed in the center of the L.A. skyline was the Angel of Independence, a well-known monument in Mexico City. On the bottom was "Tu ciudad. Tu Equipo." (Your city. Your team.) At the top it read "Los Angeles, CA," only the "CA" had been crossed out and the word "Mexico" put in its place. The message was clear: Los Angeles, Mexico.

At a U.S. versus Mexico soccer game in Los Angeles in 1998, the vast majority of the 90,000 fans were Mexican. They booed our national anthem and some tore down the American flag. The U.S. team was bombarded with all sorts of debris. Ironically, a Mexican American father and son were "pelted with beer, soda, and God knows what else for having had the temerity to display an American flag and cheer for our team."[7] Indeed, it is a rare occasion when our national soccer team plays before a pro-U.S. crowd *in this country* when competing against teams from Mexico or Central America. Former U.S.

defender Alexi Lalas summed up what it is like to constantly play before hostile fans at home:

> You don't get used to it. It stinks every time. I'm all for roots and understanding where you come from and having a respect for your homeland, but tomorrow morning all of those people are going to get up and work in the United States and live in the United States and have all the benefits of living in the United States. I would never be caught dead cheering for any other team than the United States because I know what it's given me.[8]

In Hartford, Connecticut, where 40 percent of the population is Hispanic (the largest concentration among major cities outside California, Texas, Colorado, and Florida), Spanish has become the primary language of government and is essential in many other areas. The city's web page is bilingual and if you call the mayor's office after business hours the message is first given in Spanish. Spanish is also the main language used in hospitals and banks. Mayor Eddie Perez says, "We've become a Latin city, so to speak. It's a sign of things to come."[9] Do we want Hartford to be a "Latin city," or an American city with a Latin flavor?

In yet another instance of the arrogance of our southern neighbor, the Mexican government goes out of its way to discourage the assimilation of its citizens in the United States. Juan Hernandez, the former head of Mexico's department to promote the interests of Mexicans abroad (including illegals), made this abundantly clear on ABC's *Nightline*:

> We are betting on [sic] that the Mexican American population in the United States will become more and more like the Jewish community of the United States, like the Puerto Rican community of the United States, that they will think "Mexico first" and they will invest in Mexico.... I want the third generation, the seventh generation, I want them all to think "Mexico first."[10]

American politicians and journalists have been drummed out of polite society for suggesting that Jewish Americans have dual loyalties. Yet Hernandez not only makes such a suggestion, *he sees it as a model for Mexican Americans.* Outrageous! Hernandez, by the way, is himself a dual U.S.-Mexican citizen.

Also at work here is another more bizarre factor—the legend of Aztlán. Aztlán is the mythical place of origin of the Aztec peoples, although to some it refers only to the parts of Mexico taken over by the United States after the Mexican-American War of 1846. That war is still a source of bitterness and resentment in Mexico, so much so that for many the illegal invasion of these former Mexican lands is nothing short of a "reconquista," or reconquest, of lost territories. According to Samuel Huntington, "No other immigrant group in American history has asserted or has been able to assert a historical claim to American territory. Mexicans and Mexican Americans can and do make that claim."[11]

A June 2002 Zogby poll commissioned by Americans for Immigration Control found that 58 percent of Mexicans believe the U.S. Southwest rightfully belongs to them, while 57 percent of Mexicans don't believe they need American permission to enter this country. And it doesn't help when leading politicians fan the flames, such as when former Mexican president Ernesto Zedillo told a crowd in Chicago in 1997: "I have proudly affirmed that the Mexican nation extends beyond the territory enclosed by its borders and that Mexican migrants are an important—very important—part of it."[12]

Part of the effort to extend Mexico "beyond its border" is a Mexican government initiative to encourage students to hold on to their heritage by introducing Mexican textbooks into *American* schools with large Hispanic populations. How does the Mexican government justify this outrage? According to a government spokeswoman, "We must talk about Mexican history. Our history is very rich, very intensive. It's important to know that history. *The students will feel proud to become Americans if they feel proud of their country"* (emphasis added).[13]

How they learn to feel proud about "their country" (the United States) by studying *Mexican* history isn't quite clear.

This sense among many Mexican immigrants that they are on "home" soil can be very powerful and helps explain why Mexican assimilation in these areas has always been weak—and will only get weaker as even more Mexicans move into these areas, reinforcing cultural and linguistic ties to the homeland. Essentially, immigrants are flooding these areas faster than we can assimilate them. As a result, many scholars have suggested that America's Southwest could eventually become our version of Quebec—a distinct entity within the U.S. separated from the rest of the country by ethnicity, language, and religion. Like Quebec, it could, in time, harbor strong secessionist sentiments.

Don't laugh. Charles Trujillo, a professor at the University of New Mexico, calls the secession of America's Southwest an "inevitability" because of high Hispanic immigration. He says the original Articles of Confederation gives states the right to secede and that Hispanics will use their electoral power to achieve that goal, possibly even rejoining Mexico.[14] I don't for a moment believe this is remotely possible, much less inevitable. However, after witnessing the effort to pass the Native Hawaiian Sovereignty Act, which would create a government of so-called "native" Hawaiians to exercise sovereignty over native Hawaiians living anywhere in the United States, I would not be surprised if the secession movement grows.

Trujillo is downright dispassionate compared to some on the lunatic fringe. Ernesto Cienfuegos threatens a race war in an article for *La Voz de Aztlán* (The Voice of Aztlán):

> What these bigots [who oppose illegal immigration] do not know is that they may be "opening the gates of hell" that will "unleash the rabid dogs of racial hatred." If this ever happens, it will cost all sides concerned dearly.... An escalation of anti-Mexican actions by vigilantes and militias could force a response by a large disaffected portion of our community.... The country cannot afford a serious ethnic or racial conflict in the southwest when it already has its hands full in Iraq.[15]

La Voz de Aztlán, by the way, has been designated a "hate group" by the Southern Poverty Law Center. It is perfectly natural for people to romanticize their past and hold on to their ethnic heritage. But we need those living here to be *Americans* first.

THE DANGERS OF MULTICULTURALISM

Hispanic immigrants have a harder time assimilating than other immigrant groups. It doesn't help that they are force-fed a steady diet of multiculturalism and told by their own community leaders and our own anti-American elites that America is racist, sexist, intolerant, and genocidal. And make no mistake: multiculturalism is the enemy of assimilation, and it can have devastating consequences, as we saw with the riots outside Paris and the subway bombers in London. Mark Steyn explains:

> The London bombers were, to the naked eye, assimilated—they ate fish n' chips, played cricket, sported appalling leisurewear. They'd adopted so many trees we couldn't see they lacked the big overarching forest—the essence of identity, of allegiance. As I've said before, you can't assimilate with a nullity—which is what multiculturalism is.[16]

The Islamists who rioted outside Paris last year weren't merely "disadvantaged youths" demanding more welfare. They were demanding that parts of France be recognized as Islamic territory and that French law be replaced by Islamic law, or *sharia*. They chanted "Allahou Akhbar" while torching cars. They were not and are not interested in accommodation with French society—they want to bury it. France isn't alone; other Western European countries that welcomed large numbers of Muslim immigrants without demanding that they assimilate are in the same boat. Tragically, it is too late to do anything about it now. As Dyab Abou Jahjah, the leader of the Brussels-based Arab League, says:

> We reject integration when it leads to assimilation. I don't believe in a host country. We are at home here and whatever we consider our

culture to be also belongs to our chosen country. I'm in my country, not the country of the Westerners.[17]

In his book *The West's Last Chance*, Tony Blankley quotes an equally belligerent radical German Islamist, who declares:

> Germany is an Islamic country. Islam is in the home, in schools. Germans will be outnumbered. We [Muslims] will say what we want. We'll live how we want. It's outrageous that Germans demand we speak their language. Our children will have our language, our laws, our culture.[18]

How different are these radical Islamists from the Mexican politicians who push for a Mexico without borders and undermine our efforts at assimilation? From the multiculti elites who oppose English-language education? Or from the radical left-wingers preaching "reconquista"? Arturo Vargas, executive director of the National Association of Latino Elected and Appointed Officials, declared in 1997 that changing demographics in the U.S. meant it was only a matter of time before "We shall overwhelm!" What makes his statement any less provocative than the radical Islamists quoted above?

Over three decades ago Nathan Glazer and Daniel Patrick Moynihan asked, "To what does one assimilate in modern America?"[19] In Henry Ford's day we had a great big list of things. But if multiculturalism and diversity are valued above all else, the answer is you can assimilate however you want—or not at all. It's up to you. In France they have a minister of social cohesion. How long before we need one here?

But without a strong Americanization program, the vacuum will be filled by something else. According to Heather Mac Donald, many illegal and legal Hispanic immigrants are assimilating into the same kind of underclass culture that has been so destructive to African American families:

> Hispanic teens now have the highest out-of-wedlock birth rates in the country, the highest dropout rates. . . . I've heard of the total dis-

appearance of any stigma attached to out-of-wedlock childbearing and boys now are only considered "playas" if they father children that they have no intention of supporting.... The moral of the story is that it is folly to continue with our virtual open borders policy until we've figured out a way to break the lure of underclass culture that is the real thing that people are assimilating into these days.[20]

Assimilation—and by that I mean Americanization in the early twentieth-century sense of immersing immigrants in English, American patriotism, and traditional American values—was good for immigrants and good for America. It cannot be replaced by the multicultural whim of the day. Citizenship is serious business, and we need to start treating it as such. We can begin by making English the official language of the United States, and do it now. As Teddy Roosevelt said, "We have room for but one language here, and that is the English language, for we intend to see that the crucible turns our people out as Americans."

Ironically, among the biggest supporters of acculturation and learning English are Hispanic immigrants who have successfully assimilated (think of that father and son at the soccer match). They embrace their Americanism while still holding on to their roots. They understand that English is the language of success. They are appalled at Spanish-language advocates who believe that speaking English somehow insults or dismisses their Hispanic ethnic identity.

A fascinating story in the *Arizona Republic* illustrates the growing gulf that exists between assimilated Hispanics and unassimilated newcomers in a central Phoenix neighborhood. A community action office with the Phoenix police says, "[Longtime Hispanic residents] feel like the neighborhood is being overrun by immigrants.... A lot of them are not happy with the way their neighborhood has changed." Meanwhile, the immigrants complain that assimilated Hispanics "have betrayed their country by speaking English and not celebrating the Mexican holidays." Said one, "Our Mexican Americans are even racist against our own people."[21] Doesn't that just about say it all?

Let me end this chapter with a letter I received from a constituent, a World War II veteran and member of what Tom Brokaw termed the "Greatest Generation." He wrote:

> Unrestricted immigration is destroying our sovereignty, our American culture, our traditions, and our unity as united states. We are a nation of immigrants and descendants of immigrants. The flame under our "melting pot" has gone out and our country's invasion by illegal immigrants is overwhelming assimilation. If our porous borders are not closed and all illegals deported, we shall fracture as a united nation geographically. We will always have immigration but it must be legal and strictly regulated.

To the mulitculti elites, this American hero is a bigot. To me, he is a patriot. I'm working to ensure his views—which are the views of an overwhelming majority of Americans—break through the walls of silence in Congress, where the issue of America's dissolving borders needs urgent action before we lose the country that the Greatest Generation fought to defend.

CHAPTER FOUR

LANGUAGE, POLITICAL CORRECTNESS, AND ILLEGAL IMMIGRATION

DISPATCHES FROM THE FRONT LINES

"We call things racism just to get attention. We reduce complicated problems to racism, not because it is racism, but because it works."[1]

—Immigrant "activist"
Alfredo Gutierrez

WE WERE ALL DUMBFOUNDED to learn that as a matter of policy the once venerable British Broadcasting Corporation (BBC) would not use the word "terrorist" to describe the perpetrators of the London subway bombings, opting instead for the neutral "bombers." Similarly, the policy at the Reuters news agency is not to use the word "terrorist" at all unless contained in a direct quote. Exemplifying the zeitgeist was investigative reporter Peter Taylor, who in comments about a documentary on al Qaeda he had just finished for the BBC said, "I seldom use the word terrorist, it's judgmental. If you're going to bomb trains there's probably a pretty good reason to refer to them as terrorists but I prefer not to and in [the documentary] I've said 'the London bombers.'"[2]

The abuse of language by the pro–illegal immigration crowd is just as duplicitous and just as absurd. When the *Wall Street Journal* labels anyone advocating a crackdown on illegal immigration as "anti-immigrant," it is consciously equating illegal immigration with the legal variety. But if you remove the distinction between an illegal immigrant and a legal one, if the person who sneaks across the border in violation of our laws is as much an "immigrant" as the person who has waited patiently and obeyed the rules, then the very notion of a border becomes meaningless, as does the notion of citizenship. That suits some on the Left and (sadly) even some on the Right just fine.

Another example comes from the *Arizona Republic*, which in a profile of two illegal aliens wrote, "Like most undocumented workers, Javier and Janet work aboveboard. They used fake Social Security numbers to land their jobs."[3]

Using fake Social Security numbers—a *felony*—is what passes for "aboveboard" at the politically correct *Arizona Republic*. It is hard to know whether to laugh or cry.

Even more absurd is when liberal politicians, media elites, and identity-group grievance-mongers refer to illegal aliens as "undocumented." Every time I hear that I have to laugh—not because they are being so true to form, but because the term is not even accurate.

Undocumented? Give me a break. Illegal aliens have documents galore! Social Security cards, birth certificates, work permits, driver's licenses, matrícula consular cards, or Individual Taxpayer Identification Numbers are routine. (Remember that illegal alien who got a job with the Border Patrol using a phony birth certificate?) The documents they can't obtain legally they buy on street corners.

Terrorists are even more sophisticated, producing doctored passports, phony visas, and other documents. The 1993 World Trade Center bombing mastermind Ramzi Yousef and his accomplice Ahmed Ajaj had between them five passports and numerous other documents supporting their aliases. The September 11 terrorists had thirteen driver's licenses and twenty-one other government-issued ID cards. Like their immigration papers, most of these "un"documents were "legal" in the sense that they were obtained from government authorities, albeit by fraud.

As with the use of the term "bombers," the politically correct prefer "undocumented" because it is so innocuous. They wouldn't be caught dead using the more accurate "illegal alien," not only because it *is* judgmental, but also because *they don't believe illegal aliens have done anything wrong!* To their way of thinking, the border is meaningless. One far-left group, the Border Action Network, sells T-shirts with this quote on the back: "A wall is just a wall and nothing more at all. It can be torn down." That tells you all you need to know about where they are coming from.

Democratic congressman Luis Gutierrez of Illinois, one of the sponsors of major guest worker/amnesty legislation in Congress, is as politically correct as they come, so much so that he even objects to the term "amnesty" because "there's an implication that somehow you did something wrong and you need to be forgiven."[4]

Cecilia Munoz of the National Council of La Raza doesn't approve of the word amnesty either, because "it conveys a sense of forgiving someone for a crime."[5]

And this is wishy-washy stuff compared to former Arizona state legislator and "activist" Alfredo Gutierrez, who flatly tells illegal immigrants in Arizona, "You have a right to live in this country."[6]

Mexican president Vicente Fox, who as head of state should know better, sugarcoats his countrymen's illegal invasion of the United States by deliberately mislabeling it a "migration." He refuses to call "undocumented" Mexicans "illegals," infamously telling Sean Hannity, "They are not illegals. They are not illegals. They are people that come there to work, to look for a better opportunity."[7]

Here is one of my hard and fast rules of immigration policy: anyone using the terms "undocumented" or "migrants" or "border crossers" to describe illegal aliens is more interested in accommodating illegal immigration than stopping it.

To be sure, the open-borders crowd isn't completely reticent about using judgmental language; they just save it for those opposed to the invasion of our country. The same folks who gag on the words "illegal alien" have no compunction about throwing around such terms as "racist," "xenophobic," and other epithets to describe their opponents.

Vicente Fox has called U.S. border control efforts in San Diego and Texas "discriminatory."[8] He said those of us opposed to illegal immigration are part of "minority, xenophobic, discriminatory groups."[9] All this hectoring and lecturing on race from the man who declared that illegals in the United States "take work that not even blacks want to do."

Even the Catholic Church is not above playing the race card. Although I'm not Catholic, I have the utmost respect for the church and its teachings, so much so that I send my daughter to a Catholic high school. So I was more than a little disappointed to read some of the comments made when the U.S. Conference of Catholic Bishops launched its campaign in support of amnesty for illegal aliens. Commenting on what he called the "migration phenomenon"—but what the rest of us would call the "illegal invasion"—Bishop James A. Tamayo of the Diocese of Laredo said, "Our experience on the border is far from the vision of the Kingdom of God that Jesus proclaimed: many who seek to migrate are suffering, and, in some cases, tragically dying; communities are divided; and racist and xenophobic attitudes remain."[10]

While well-meaning, the bishops' campaign is sanctimony masquerading as policy. The bishops blame the United States for illegals dying in the desert when they should blame Mexico, which does not offer these people economic opportunity at home and actively encourages them to cross the deserts and deal with dangerous "coyotes" to illegally enter the country. The bishops insult Americans by calling them "anti-immigrant" when they are "anti-*illegal* immigrant." Not once do they acknowledge that illegal aliens might be doing something wrong. Their solution? Open the borders.

Samuel Johnson once said that patriotism is the last refuge of scoundrels. In the debate on illegal immigration, racism is the last refuge of liberals who have run out of arguments.

Republican congressman Tom Tancredo of Colorado is one of the most passionate advocates of ending illegal immigration. When he offered an amendment to deny federal funds to cities with sanctuary policies, liberals on the House floor responded with their usual paranoid ravings:[11]

- "[Tancredo] wants all of us who look a certain way, who have certain names and speak a certain way to have Big Brother filter us out."—Democrat Bob Menendez of New Jersey

- "This amendment, in my opinion, would make Osama bin Laden proud."—Democrat Joe Crowley of New York
- "The gentleman from Colorado [Mr. Tancredo] with this amendment declares war on Los Angeles and a number of other cities throughout this country!"—Democrat Howard Berman of California

Of course, I get my fair share of name-calling too. One writer called me *"retrasadas mentales"* (mentally retarded)[12] because I think we should make English our nation's official language. The lieutenant governor of Iowa, Sally Pederson, said I was part of a group of "single issues radicals who share extreme and discriminatory views of immigration."[13] Another columnist, Salvador Reza, a so-called human rights activist, accused me of having a "hatred" of Mexican children before becoming totally unhinged:

If a child is Mexican and can't speak English even the laws turn against him/her. That child will be subjected to sanctions and psychological torture for being Mexican under the color of law. They endure a treatment only equaled by the treatment of native Americans at the beginning of the century under the Boarding School Americanization projects.[14]

As the kids today would say: whatever, dude.

Believe it or not, the media in Arizona take this guy seriously. But this is the kind of hysteria that has, sadly, become the norm when debating illegal immigration.

Naturally, it wouldn't be a real goofball movement without Hollywood getting in on the act. In a February 2005 ad in *Daily Variety*, some three dozen of the usual Tinseltown suspects urged California governor Arnold Schwarzenegger to sign legislation allowing illegal immigrants to get California driver's licenses. Conservative columnist Debra Saunders had some fun quoting one of the signers, Mike Farrell of *M*A*S*H* fame:

"We give them access to our homes. We trust them with our children. It seems absurd to me to not grant them the respect they deserve," Farrell explained to Copley News Service.

What's this "we" business? Most people don't hire nannies. Only rich people can afford nannies; they can hire legal nannies.[15]

M*A*S*H alumna Loretta Swit ("Hot Lips" Houlihan) also lent her name to the cause. However, *M*A*S*H* character Charles Emerson Winchester III, who I'm sure knows a thing or two about hired help, was nowhere to be found, which is understandable since in one episode he muttered, "My family has been having problems with immigrants ever since we came to America!"

The liberals never miss an opportunity to play the race card. What is galling is when folks who should know better do it. One of the worst examples was when the *Wall Street Journal* took former Wyoming senator Alan Simpson to task because he proposed an increase in legal immigration of "only" 35 percent. The *Journal* even compared him to former Klan leader David Duke![16]

And it's not just the *Journal*. At a House Republican retreat in West Virginia, I talked to President George W. Bush's closest adviser, Karl Rove. I told him that I had spoken to the president about why I thought it would be a mistake to submit to Congress the totalization agreement that has been signed with Mexico (coordinating our Social Security system with theirs). The president thanked me for being candid and said he would consider my views. But Rove became somewhat exasperated and spluttered, "You just don't want to help brown people, do you?"

I had to pinch myself. Had I taken a wrong turn somewhere on the way to West Virginia? Was this the president's right-hand man, or had I stumbled into the *Twilight Zone*? One thing is certain: we don't need Republicans playing the race card when there are so many liberals who are so good at it.

But some on our side are fighting back, and it can't happen too soon. And if you ever wanted to know what happens when the Left gets a little taste of its own medicine, take at look at what transpired in the city of Baldwin Park, California.

WELCOME TO BALDWIN PARK— NOW GET THE HELL OUT!

In June 2005, Baldwin Park, nearly 80 percent Hispanic, was embroiled in a controversy of its own making. At the Metrolink station stands a monument called "Danza Indigenas," a twenty-foot-tall arch that, according to L.A.'s Metropolitan Transportation Authority, is supposed to "trace the historical importance of the California Mission period to contemporary Baldwin Park."[17] Designed by muralist Judy Baca, this monument to political correctness was dedicated in 1993 and sits on public land and was paid for with taxpayer dollars. There is even a plaque from the mayor.

Above the several arches are various quotes, two of which proved highly, and rightly, controversial:

- "It was better before *they* came."
- "This land was Mexican once, was Indian always and is, and will be again."

A California-based anti–illegal immigration group, Save Our State (SOS), organized protests in Baldwin Park in an effort to get the city to remove what its members deemed to be these "racist" and "seditious" inscriptions. Counter-protesters—usually outnumbering those from SOS—carried signs and banners and wore T-shirts touting the usual left-wing sentiments. Among the predictably idiotic slogans were these beauts:

- "All Europeans are illegal on this continent since 1492"
- "One world for the workers without borders"
- "F*ck the Minutemen, F*ck the S.O.S., F*ck the police too"
- "Racists get out of Aztlán"

The protests often turned heated, though not violent. But one elderly woman—an SOS supporter—was struck in the head with a water bottle and taken to the hospital. She is suing Baldwin Park.

Ironically, Baca says that the quote "It was better before *they* came" (from a poem by Gloria Anzaldúa) actually refers to jeers uttered by whites against Mexican immigrants who began moving into Baldwin Park after World War II. What this has to do with the California Mission period is anyone's guess. In any event, the quote is provocative and racist no matter how you read it.

The gold medal for irony, however, has to go to the mayor of Baldwin Park, Manuel Lozano. In a story about one protest, the *Los Angeles Times* reported: "'Baldwin Park has never, ever in its history seen anything like this. The residents want these outsiders out of our city,' said Mayor Manuel Lozano, who wants the city to send Save Our State members a bill for the costs of dealing with the protests. The mayor added, 'I feel our city is under siege.'"[18]

Fed-up Americans who feel their *country* is "under siege" by illegal aliens, who really are "outsiders," are branded racists and bigots. Ditto for Americans who want to send Mexico a bill for the costs of caring for its citizens. All of which escapes the clueless mayor, who, far from being embarrassed by the racist inscriptions, actually organized a ceremony in which he presented the artist with a city resolution declaring the monument a part of the city's history!

The inscriptions on the monument were, to say the least, poorly chosen and they shame the city of Baldwin Park. There is no way the offending inscriptions "honor" any group, whatever the intent of the artist. The message is simply one of resentment and bitterness. But if that's the impression the people of Baldwin Park want to convey to "outsiders," it is their choice. Just don't be surprised when some of those "outsiders," better known as American citizens, take exception and exercise their First Amendment rights in response.

THE MINUTEMEN: HEROES OR VIGILANTES?

For case studies in out-of-control political correctness, however, nothing beats the case of the Minuteman Project.

In April 2005, the Minuteman Project patrolled a twenty-three-mile stretch of the Arizona-Mexico border. Their goal was to focus national attention on our scandalously porous southern border. Like many, I admit to being a little wary of the Minutemen at first. Opposing illegal immigration is not a racist cause, and I was concerned that if the group were infiltrated by white supremacists or other extreme elements it would end up doing the cause more harm than good, no matter how many other good people were involved. Minuteman organizers Chris Simcox and James Gilchrist gave strong assurances that the operation would be peaceful and that they were doing their best to make certain the group was free of anyone who might cause trouble. They also insisted the group would operate under strict guidelines: do not confront illegals, do not apprehend illegals, and do not draw your weapon (if you have one) unless absolutely necessary.

I decided to withhold judgment until I could check them out for myself. Others weren't quite so circumspect. Weeks before the operation even began, the liberals were in full circus mode:

- The *Arizona Republic* editorialized: "[T]his is more about Deputy Dawg than effecting change. Law enforcement doesn't need or want a bunch of armed good ol' boys getting in the way of a dangerous job." It added that the citizen protesters were a "bunch of soldier-of-fortune wannabes."[19]
- Ray Ybarra, a spokesman for the ACLU of Arizona, warned that the Minutemen could "come to our state as vigilantes and end up leaving as defendants." The ACLU trained its people to shadow the Minuteman volunteers to make sure they didn't violate anyone's rights.[20] (Some ACLU volunteers were reportedly caught on tape smoking marijuana, which explains a lot.)
- Miguel Escobar Valdez, the Mexican consul in Douglas, Arizona, said: "The Mexican army is on alert. Also, law enforcement will be vigilant because the situation is very volatile."[21]
- Armando Navarro, a University of California–Riverside political science professor and coordinator of the National Alliance

for Human Rights, said, "They are domestic terrorists that represent a danger to the country and could promote a major border conflict that will have serious ramifications and consequences."[22] He went on to say that although his group would use nonviolent tactics to confront the Minutemen, "We will adjust to the situation, and obviously some of us have experience in the military."[23]

Unlike most of the armchair critics, I made it a point to visit the border during the operation to see for myself what the Minutemen were all about. I visited their headquarters and toured the operations center and radio room. I talked to reporters who had been covering the operation from the beginning. I met with local political leaders and law enforcement. I talked to the Minuteman leadership and volunteers sitting in pickup truck beds and lawn chairs all along the line. These were not the "yahoos" depicted by some in the media. They were patriotic citizens, well organized and media savvy. Every state was represented in their ranks, from the bluest blue to the reddest red. They were young and old, black and white, men and women. And they were effective.

The Border Patrol reported a large drop in apprehensions along the sector patrolled by the Minutemen for the month of the operation. Predictably, there was an attendant surge in activity in other sectors, which stands to reason. Just as illegals avoid stepped-up security at the San Diego and El Paso sectors, they would naturally avoid the Minutemen. The liberal media pointed to this as proof that the Minutemen were ineffective. Actually, it proved that with sufficient will and resources, we can secure the border.

Of course, federal officials were none too pleased with the Minutemen, but even I was taken back by the pettiness of what happened afterward. Besides being a co-founder of the Minutemen, Chris Simcox was at the time also editor and owner of a newspaper in Tombstone, Arizona. Shortly after the Minuteman operation ended, Simcox received an advisory for a press conference Department of Homeland Security secretary Michael Chertoff would be having in Douglas, Arizona. When he attempted to enter the building with his press credentials, the Border Patrol agents wouldn't let him in, telling him it was for "security reasons." If only crossing our border were so difficult!

Since everyone seemed so concerned about the Minutemen being armed—I personally saw very few who were—I was especially eager to find out what the truth was. I talked with a radio reporter from Phoenix who had been "embedded" with the Minutemen for most of the month. He told me that he and a newspaper reporter from California decided to count the number of armed Minutemen they saw (it is legal in Arizona to carry a sidearm). After comparing notes, they decided that it was only 15 to 20 percent, hardly the armed mob we were warned about.

In fact, it turns out that the Minutemen were less armed than most other Arizonans. Surveys show that a third of Arizonans own guns, although polling I've done in my districts puts it closer to a half. (It takes me back to what a campaign volunteer from the Northeast once said to me: "I've finally figured out why everyone in Arizona is so friendly. You're all carrying guns!")

As to the number of shots fired during the entire month: zero. In fact, I don't know of a single instance in which a Minuteman even drew a gun, despite numerous provocations.

Area residents and reporters told me that some members of the press dressed up as illegal aliens and crept around the desert at night, hoping to goad the Minutemen. It didn't work. In fact, the worst that happened was one illegal alien, after being given lifesaving food and water, was asked to pose for a photograph holding a T-shirt that read, "Bryan Barton Caught Me Crossing the Border and All I Got Was This Lousy T-Shirt." The Minutemen immediately expelled Barton.

Barton's was a juvenile, but harmless, stunt. Still, the Arizona ACLU responded with its usual rhetorical excess, intoning: "In a nation of laws, this is intolerable."[24] Drug and human smugglers illegally cross our border at will, and the ACLU finds some goofy prank "intolerable"? And let's remember that only one party in the T-shirt kerfuffle broke the law—the illegal alien!

Maybe the ACLU wanted us to feel sorry for the illegal because he might have been embarrassed holding up that shirt. He should have been. He foolishly broke the law, got caught, and almost died from hunger and dehydration in the process. I would think that's enough even to embarrass an ACLU member. In any event, the day the ACLU declares millions of illegal aliens "intolerable" is maybe the day we'll take it seriously when it lectures us on being "a nation of laws."

The media firestorm reached its zenith when California governor Arnold Schwarzenegger expressed support for the Minutemen and called for securing the border (he originally advocated the "closure" of the border, but later clarified that he meant "securing" it). Thirty-two state governors from Mexico wrote to Schwarzenegger, accusing him of "encouraging xenophobia and exalting the use of force" and offering "support to a group of armed civilians." That's not all; they said that Schwarzenegger's position "threatens the most elementary human rights and the avenues established between nations to resolve problems that might place at risk the security and stability of the region." And then they subtly reminded him that California has the greatest number of Mexicans in the United States.[25]

The Minutemen were constantly portrayed as trigger-happy, gun-toting crazies, yet it was the ACLU, Mexican officials, and radical supporters of illegal immigration who kept threatening armed conflict. Just who were the real yahoos?

But the hands-down winner for elitist condescension and gratuitous insult goes to Sarah Vowell, who in a column for the *New York Times* wrote the following about the spread of the Minuteman Project to other states:

Americans now have to fret for the safety of these clowns, who have been condemned by President Bush as "vigilantes." Because, odds are, the only people they'll end up shooting will be one another. And I say that not only as a namby-pamby liberal writing for the most uppity newspaper in the world, but also as the daughter of a gunsmith, a man who was so persnickety about the very real danger of firearms' tendency to just go off that he practically made my sister and me don hunter orange just to play with squirt guns.[26]

Despite the "tendency" of guns to "just go off," not one did along the Arizona-Mexico border in April. Do you think maybe the Minutemen have discovered a way to suppress this tendency, such as not pulling the trigger?

Equally idiotic is the liberal Vowell's intimation that she knows more about firearms than the kind of "clowns" who join the Minutemen— you know, like all those retired military and law enforcement personnel. Next thing you know, Vowell will be telling us that namby-pamby liberals are better at winning elections.

Even President Bush was taken in by the hyperbole of the left-wing activist groups and editorial writers denouncing the Minutemen. Before the first lawn chair was unfolded, he told reporters, "I'm against vigilantes in the United States of America. I'm for enforcing law in a rational way. That's why we got a border patrol. And they ought to be in charge of enforcing the border."[27]

Just hours later, the president welcomed to his ranch Mexican president Vicente Fox, who called the Minutemen "migrant hunters" but who calls Mexican illegals "heroes."

At a press conference in Washington at the end of the operation, I said of the Minuteman Project:

> These are extraordinary Americans from all walks of life who followed their constitutional right to petition their government for redress of a grievance, in this case, the abject failure of the federal government to secure our border. And for that simple constitutional act of standing up for border security these citizens were maligned far and wide by hysterical editorial writers and yes, sadly, even by the presidents of the United States and the Republic of Mexico.

I then called on the president to issue an apology to the Minutemen for maligning them. The White House refused.

As long as the White House sees the Minutemen as part of the problem and Vicente Fox as part of the solution, we will never get anywhere on illegal immigration. As we will see, Fox and the entire Mexican government are accessories to the illegal invasion of our country. (Rumors at the border were that the Mexican army and Grupos Beta— a specially trained Mexican force that offers advice and assistance to border crossers—were transporting illegal crossers to sectors not being patrolled by the Minutemen.) Bush should have invited the Minutemen to his ranch and left Fox cooling his heels in Mexico City.

Predictably, the American people had a very different view of the Minutemen than the elites did. A statewide poll found that 57 percent of Arizonans supported the Minuteman Project while only 34 percent opposed it.[28]

In an editorial after the conclusion of the Minuteman Project, the *Arizona Republic* commented, "Commendably, there were no ugly confrontations, no displays of vigilantism that some feared."[29] Of course, the *Arizona Republic* itself was part of the "some" who "feared." But in the end even mushy-headed editorial writers had to agree that the Minutemen turned out to be just what they said they were—ordinary Americans concerned about illegal immigration who wanted to send a strong message to their government. In that they surely succeeded.

DEMOCRATS' DIRTY TRICKS

Believe me when I say that it doesn't take much to get the Left's "Republicans are racist" machinery in motion. I have experienced it firsthand. Here's the story.

In February 2002 I took to the House floor to speak in support of an amendment to ban noncitizens from making political contributions to candidates and political parties. The fund-raising scandals involving members of the Red Chinese intelligence services making illegal contributions to the Clinton-Gore campaign in 1996 were still fresh in my mind. In my view, the actions of the Clinton-Gore team were utterly inexcusable, bordering on treasonous, and I wanted to make sure that nothing like that could ever happen again.

Here is the entire version of the short speech I gave that day. It has not been altered in any way and it is important that you see it in its entirety.

I thank my friend from Mississippi and the chairman of the committee of the whole House, and I thank my friend from Hawaii for her impassioned statement.

You know the whole purpose of the amendment process is to offer perfecting amendments, and indeed if we follow the gentle lady's logic, then we would allow noncitizens to vote.

After all, shouldn't they have a voice? Indeed, we've seen evidence of that in recent election campaigns. Just as we saw in 1996, Bernard Schwartz, the leading contributor to the Democratic Party and his Loral missile systems, give the Communist Chinese guidance systems, and our commander in chief at that time did absolutely nothing. And that was an outrage.

But we understand the pop psychology of the Left, it's "Oh gee, it's just this horrible system. I didn't really mean it. It's just a horrible system."

Well, now, my friends, here is your chance to change the system. To say, lawful citizens can contribute. No more financiers of Red Pagoda Communist Chinese cigarettes; no more daughters of the head of the Chinese equivalent of the CIA who showed up in the Oval Office; no more sham corporations, Chinese shell corporations operated by the Red Army of China, doing their dirty work through soft money to a Clinton-Gore reelection campaign.

If you're serious about reform, stand up for national security, stand up for this perfecting amendment. But I know the Orwellian phrase will be, somehow this is a poison pill. Yes, I guess it is poisonous to disallow enemies of this state access to our political system.

That is so bizarre. Shame on those who advocate this. Support this amendment. Stand up for America. Improve the system.

It was a tough, but fair, speech on an important topic. What happened next is too bizarre for words.

In a cynical attempt to score points with Hispanic voters, the Democratic Congressional Campaign Committee (DCCC) issued a press release about my speech headlined, "GOP Says Hispanics Are 'Enemies of the State,' Democrats Fight Back." I'm not making this up.

The release began, "Yesterday, during a debate on the floor of the United States House of Representatives, Arizona Republican J. D. Hayworth likened Hispanic legal permanent residents to 'enemies of the state.'" Later in the release left-wing congressman Bob Menendez added, "Rep. Hayworth's comment is the latest attack on the Hispanic community by the Republican leadership in Congress."[30]

These outrageous assertions are obviously belied by the transcript—in which, as you can see, the word Hispanic does not appear (while the Communist Chinese are mentioned four times).

But the DCCC has never let the truth get in the way of a good smear. In a propaganda stunt worthy of the old Soviet Union, the Democrats put a *doctored* audio track of my speech on their website. All my references to the Communist Chinese efforts on behalf of the Clinton-Gore campaign, the main thrust of the speech, were conveniently edited out. All that was left was my plea not to let "enemies of this state" have access to our political system.[31]

That's not all. The *Washington Post* decided to get in on the act. My office played an audio recording of the entire speech for *Post* reporter Juliet Eilperin, and this is what was written the next day in Lloyd Grove's "Reliable Source" column:

Depending on one's point of view, Hayworth first insulted Chinese Americans, then violated House rules with a slur on a fellow congressman. Around 1 a.m., Hayworth ended a peroration about illegal Chinese campaign contributions by implying that letting legal foreign residents write checks would give "enemies of the state access to our political system." The comment prompted Rep. David Wu (D-Ore.), a Chinese American, to say that Hayworth "has perpetrated a great evil."[32]

Great evil? David Wu obviously wouldn't know a "great evil" if it bit him on the...never mind. But when it comes to inciting racial division, he is a pro.

So according to the DCCC and Bob Menendez, I was attacking Hispanics; according to David Wu I was attacking Chinese Americans. While the Democrats couldn't agree among themselves just who I was attacking, they were sure it was someone other than those I specifically singled out in my speech—the Communist Chinese involved in the Clinton-Gore fund-raising scandal!

On my behalf, my chief of staff wrote to Lloyd Grove and Juliet Eilperin, saying, among other things, that "since the amendment in question had to do with foreigners (legal resident aliens) getting access to our political system and since the congressman's comments were clearly directed at members of a hostile foreign power (the PRC), how could you with a clear conscience even hint that his remarks were directed at any group of *Americans*?"

How indeed. But this appeal to the reporters' sense of fair play was an utterly futile gesture. Why? Because one of the ironclad lessons I have learned from my years in the media and dealing with them as a member of Congress is that the majority of the liberal reporters who dominate the elite media have a far greater dedication to writing a story that fits their prejudices than to writing a fair, balanced, *factual* story that does not comport with their liberal views.

Now for the cherry on top. In the DCCC's press release I cited above, Bob Menendez ripped Republicans for even offering the amendment that prohibited noncitizens from making contributions to political campaigns—the one I spoke in favor of. He called it an "attempt to silence voices and exclude ethnic groups." Yet on March 30, 1998, Menendez voted "aye" on the Illegal Foreign Contributions Act of 1998, which would have—you guessed it!—barred noncitizens from making campaign contributions or expenditures.

Bob Menendez is no doubt a hypocrite and a phony to boot. But if the Left will go to such extremes over an issue concerning whether legal resident aliens, who are not even citizens after all, should be allowed to make political contributions, you can only imagine what they have in store for us as the debate on illegal immigration heats up.

INTIMIDATION IS FOR LOSERS

These outrages notwithstanding, I won't be intimidated. I swore an oath to uphold and defend the Constitution. It is an oath I take seriously. I have no doubt that when this book is published, I will be pilloried by the elite media—and even by some Republicans. But when it comes to our border security and illegal immigration, I will not be cowed into inaction because of what "namby-pamby" editorial writers at the *New York Times* or the *Wall Street Journal* or even Karl Rove might say.

America's survival instinct has taken a back seat to rampant political correctness and multicultural sensibilities have trumped national security. Little old ladies are frisked in airports so we don't offend young Muslim men from terrorist-sponsoring Middle Eastern countries. American citizens peacefully assemble to patrol the border and the grievance-mongers scream racism.

Terrorists kill 3,000 of us and we are told the real question is not "where do we bomb first?" but "why do they hate us?" Illegal aliens invade our country with the active encouragement of a foreign government and they tell us the question isn't "how do we get them to leave?" but "how can we make them feel welcome?" We act like a bunch of defeatist wimps unwilling to stand up for our culture, our borders, our security, or our own laws.

I refuse to accept that. We would be foolish to sacrifice our national security on the altar of political correctness. After all, what could possibly be correct about *illegal* immigration?

CHAPTER FIVE

MEXICO: FRIEND OR FOE?

"According to a new study by National Geographic, *11 percent of Americans between the ages of eighteen and twenty-four could not find the United States on a map of the world. You know the only place where everyone could find the United States on a map? Mexico."*

—Jay Leno, on the *Tonight Show*

MEXICAN PRESIDENT Vicente Fox says he loves America. Apparently, he loves it so much he wants to run it. At the very least, he wants to be the one to set our immigration policies. We would be fools to let him.

Fox's ultimate goal is an open border that would allow "a free flow of people" between the United States and Mexico, although I have a feeling that the "flow" would be mostly one way. Since the September 11, 2001, terror attacks, Fox has had to put his plans for an officially open border on hold. But that hasn't stopped him from mounting an assault on our sovereignty by encouraging more Mexicans to head north, not only breaking our immigration laws, but also trampling the spirit of citizenship and assimilation those laws were designed to foster.

Exhibit A is the *Guide for the Mexican Migrant*, of which 1.5 million copies were distributed as a free supplement to *El Libro Vaquero*, a popular cowboy comic book. Produced by Mexico's Foreign Ministry, the guide was supposedly intended to give some "practical advice that could be of use if you already have made the difficult decision to seek new job opportunities outside your country." Of course, the "practical advice" did not include information on how to go about entering the United States legally, but did include other useful information about the best way to cross the border without being detected. In reality, it was nothing but a how-to manual for illegal entry into America.

In response, I wrote a letter of protest to the Mexican ambassador. His government's continued encouragement of its citizens to break America's immigration laws is, I wrote, "nothing less than an act of deliberate hostility against the United States—an attack on our sovereignty." I also stated that "it must cease before it does permanent damage to our relationship." The ambassador responded that the purpose of the guide was to "avoid the loss of lives" and that "the Government of Mexico does not encourage undocumented immigration to the United States."

Baloney.

Besides tips for crossing the border safely, the guide goes further by providing illegals with recommendations for evading detection of authorities *once inside the United States*. It warns, "Avoid attracting attention," and advises that "The best formula is not to alter your routine at work or at home." And, like the parents of teenagers, it recommends, "Avoid loud parties. The neighbors might get annoyed and call the police."

That advice isn't about saving lives: it's about not getting caught!

And how do you suppose the ambassador would square his ridiculous claim that his government doesn't encourage illegal immigration with the following bit of advice to would-be illegals from Ernesto Ruffo Appel, Mexico's commissioner for Northern Border Affairs? *"If the Border Patrol finds you, try again."*[1]

And the United States is supposed to be the arrogant one in this relationship?

When the September 11 attacks put an end to whatever hope he had of getting an amnesty agreement out of Washington, Fox decided to take matters into his own hands by offering the "matrícula consular" identity cards. The card contains the holder's name, date and place of birth, current address, a current photograph, and signature. As a form of ID, it is a joke—and a dangerous one at that. The FBI says the card is "not a reliable form of identification" and could be used by terrorists to establish phony identities in the United States.[2] In fact, federal officials have discovered individuals from many different countries in possession of what are supposedly "Mexican" ID cards. Since someone here legally already has proper identification, only illegal aliens need matrículas. They make it easy for illegal aliens to open bank accounts and get a driver's license, a breeder document that is de facto amnesty.

And when we do stick up for ourselves, watch out! In May 2005, President Bush signed into law the REAL ID Act, which requires states to stop providing illegal aliens with driver's licenses and thus hamper criminal aliens and terrorists from traveling freely in our country. This did not go over well with the Mexican government.

Foreign Minister Luis Ernesto Derbez announced that his country would take its complaints against U.S. immigration policy to the United Nations. Meanwhile, Fox said Mexico would issue a formal complaint against the law, which he said was incompatible with "the harmonious development of relations between the United States and Mexico."[3]

Santiago Creel, Mexico's interior secretary, called the law "negative, inconvenient, and obstructionist,"[4] three terms that could probably be applied to every law in the U.S. Code!

The REAL ID Act also waived environmental rules that had prevented completion of the last section of the fence along the border near San Diego, again causing much ire in Mexico. More Creel: "Building walls doesn't help anyone build a good neighborhood."[5]

The Mexican interior ministry is apparently not familiar with the American aphorism "Good fences make good neighbors." Good neighbors respect one another's property. After what you read earlier about the physical state of our border, can Creel claim with a straight face that Mexico respects ours?

The sad fact is that successive Mexican governments have found it easier—preferable, really—to actively encourage illegal entry into the United States rather than to fix Mexico's ailing economy and the corruption endemic throughout all layers of Mexican society. Mexico acts as an accomplice in illegal immigration because its economy is hooked on the $17 billion in annual remittances from Mexicans working in the

U.S.—more than it earns from tourism or foreign investment and perhaps economically more important than its state-owned oil industry. Nearly one in five Mexicans receives remittances from relatives working in the United States. Mexican towns use this money for infrastructure repairs or other public projects that the Mexican government cannot—or will not—do.

Earlier I mentioned OTMs, the classification of illegal immigrants who are "other than Mexican." As far as the Mexican government is concerned, every one of its citizens here illegally is an *ATM*, a mini cash machine for an economy in perpetual trouble. As author Luis Alberto Urrea says, "Mexico's government has become a crack whore, tragically selling its youth cheaply for its substance of choice, the long green."[6]

Because they provide this economic lifeline to the Mexican economy, illegals have been heralded as "heroes" by Vicente Fox.[7] Indeed, the Mexican government routinely honors expatriates, as it did in December 2004 when the first "Day of the Yucatecan Migrant"[8] was held. In fact, Mexican expatriates, legal and illegal (including dual citizens), have become such a potent political force that Mexico recently passed a law making an estimated four million Mexicans in the United States eligible to vote in Mexico's upcoming presidential election. (This gesture comes too late, as they've already voted with their feet by leaving!)

But Mexico's encouragement of illegal immigration is shortsighted. Losing millions of its hardest-working people to the lure of an American job has had a devastating impact on that country. There are whole villages comprised almost entirely of women, children, and old men because all the young men have headed north to work. The mayor of Santa Ana Del Valle in Oaxaca says, "Approximately half the town is [in the U.S.] now. We're left with empty houses."[9] That can't be good for Mexico's long-term economic, social, or cultural health.

And yet, even with all this, I read the following in an op-ed piece by the consul general of Mexico, Francisco J. Alejo: "We know that Mexico loses when its hard-working people leave our country."[10]

Give me a break! The Mexican government does everything but parachute its people into our country, and then officials shed crocodile tears because they are leaving. How do you say "chutzpah" in Spanish?

MEXICO'S A-MAIZING HYPOCRISY

Can you imagine what the reaction would be in Mexico if the roles were reversed? The following story will give you some idea.

A couple of years ago the Mexican government became upset when some biotech corn produced in the United States was found growing in fields in Mexico. No one is sure how the corn came to be planted, but a report by a panel chosen by the North American Free Trade Agreement (NAFTA) suspects that Mexican farmers took "officially legal and sanctioned"[11] corn from the U.S. that was supposed to be ground into cornmeal and planted it instead. Still, as expected, America was assailed.

One American member of the NAFTA-appointed panel made this point: "Like us, [the Mexicans] have the right to make up their own minds about genetically modified crops."[12]

Let me make sure I understand. We're supposed to respect the Mexican border when it comes to corn (and we do), but they don't have to respect our border when it comes to people?

The report also contains this gem:

> Many campesinos and the community organizers who are most vocal and concerned with transgenic gene flow perceive [genetically modified corn] as a direct threat to *political autonomy, cultural identity, personal safety* and biodiversity [emphasis added].[13]

Americans concerned with those very same issues regarding illegal aliens on this side of the border are labeled bigots and xenophobes by the Mexican government and many in the elite media; similar feelings by campesinos in Mexico about *corn*—perfectly safe corn at that—are treated with the utmost gravity. I believe the Mexican people have the right to decide what kind and how much corn they want coming into their country. I just as strongly believe we have the right to determine who and how many people come into our country.

Because Mexico won't take the steps necessary to open up its statist economy, it looks to the United States to soak up its excess labor. And we have. The 1986 amnesty conferred green cards on about 2.5 million Mexicans. Every year about 210,000 Mexicans are allowed into America legally, three times more than we take from any other country. It is now estimated that there are no fewer than five million Mexicans living here illegally. America has been a tolerant and generous neighbor in this regard. But enough is enough.

Mexico could use a stern lecture from President Bush about its state sponsorship of illegal immigration, which is nothing less than a deliberate attack on American sovereignty. Sadly, neither the president nor any officials in his administration are willing to confront the Mexicans. In fact, the president bends over backwards to promote his Mexican counterpart.

Bush's reluctance to push Fox too hard is partly understandable from the standpoint of "regional stability." As bad as Vicente Fox is, he and his right-leaning National Action Party may be better than any of the alternatives. Still, it is hard to believe that the situation could get any worse. We've been looking the other way for decades as Mexico makes a mockery of our laws, with nothing to show for it except higher crime, hospital closures, lower wages, and a disrespect for the rule of law. In testimony before the Senate, Mark K. Reed, a former Border Patrol agent and currently the CEO and president of an immigration and border security consulting firm in Tucson, Arizona, related this stunning anecdote that says it all:

Almost twenty years ago President [George H. W.] Bush declared the War on Drugs. I was present at a high-level strategy meeting between representatives of federal law enforcement, DoD [Department of Defense], and the State Department regarding the urgency of sealing the Mexican border to stop drug smuggling. When DoD stated that they were capable of detecting and interdicting any intrusion, but could not distinguish between groups of migrants from drug smugglers until interdiction, the dialogue became difficult. When DoD refused to entertain the idea that they should only detain drug smugglers upon interdiction, the meeting was abruptly terminated. The safety valve that illegal immigration provided toward the stability of Mexico seemed to be a more compelling national security priority than drug smuggling.[14]

Haven't we learned anything from our experience in the Middle East, where we have paid a terrible price for a decades-long policy based on "stability" and "realism"? Franklin Delano Roosevelt once said about the brutal Nicaraguan dictator and U.S. ally Anastasio Somoza, "He may be a sonofabitch, but he's our sonofabitch." That theory made sense when the alternative was Communism, but makes no sense now. As Mark Steyn put it, "The problem with the SOB theory of geopolitical management—he may be a sonofabitch but he's our sonofabitch—is that the reverse is more to the point: he may be our sonofabitch but in the end he's a sonofabitch."[15]

George W. Bush has with great courage and perception changed our Middle East policy to one based on spreading democracy, stopping corruption, encouraging modernization, and promoting economic progress. Likewise, we need to do more to *strongly* encourage Mexico to clean up its act.

Back in 1986, when Congress was debating the Immigration Reform and Control Act, it was said that both nations benefited from illegal immigration. The United States got a steady supply of cheap labor while Mexico got an "escape valve" to relieve pressure because it could not create enough decent jobs at decent wages for a growing population. Here we are twenty years later and *nothing has changed.* One might reasonably ask what the Mexican government has been doing all that time to improve its economy. The short answer is: not nearly enough, because its people keep right on coming.

DOES MEXICO'S ECONOMY WORK?

One thing we can say for sure about Mexico's economy is that all of its problems are self-inflicted. Mexico is a large country rich in natural resources with a large, hard-working population. It sits next door to, and has a free trade agreement (NAFTA) with, the largest economy in the world and a natural market for its products.

Given these advantages, there is no legitimate reason why the Mexican economy should not be able to provide adequate jobs for its people. As scholar George Grayson put it, "If Singapore could lease Mexico for twenty years, Americans soon would be complaining about the 'colossus of the South.'"

According to the CIA's World Factbook, Mexico's gross domestic product (GDP) recently passed the trillion-dollar threshold. By that simple measure Mexico is the fourteenth largest economy in the world. However, on a GDP per capita basis, Mexico is stuck in the middle of the pack, at eighty-fifth.

In the 2004 presidential election John Kerry repeatedly leveled the false charge that the United States was in a "jobless recovery." If he wanted to see what a jobless recovery really looks like, he should have looked south of the border.

In 2004 the Mexican economy grew by 4.1 percent, the stock market surged by almost 50 percent, inflation was held to 4.9 percent, and the peso remained relatively stable. It stands poised to do even better, especially if oil prices remain high. However, this solid economic performance has not translated into jobs for the Mexican people because of institutional and structural restraints that keep the Mexican economy on the brink of third-world status instead of allowing it to reach its powerhouse potential.

For example, Mexico's state-owned oil company—Petroleo Mexicanos, or Pemex—is the largest company in Latin America. It is also the world's third largest producer of crude oil and the number-two supplier of oil to the United States, behind Canada but ahead of Saudi Arabia.

But Pemex is in trouble. Since it pays the Mexican government about sixty cents of every dollar in sales, it doesn't have the resources to modernize its pipelines and refineries or make the necessary investments in exploration or production.

Mexico has the fourth-highest proven crude reserves in the Western hemisphere, but lacks the resources to get at it. Mexico has natural gas deposits that are likely bigger than those in the U.S. or Canada, but can't produce enough gas to meet its own needs!

That's because Pemex is not only a cash cow for the government, it is a sacred cow as well. The Mexican constitution restricts exploration, production, development, and final sales to Pemex only. Vicente Fox has tried to circumvent constitutional restrictions, but oil nationalism in Mexico runs so deep that even minor changes are nearly impossible.

As a result, energy-rich Mexico must import natural gas and refined petroleum products. It is even looking to import electricity from the United States. Former Pemex chief Francisco Rojas summed it up this way: "We have a strange notion of sovereignty in Mexico. We now rely on the U.S. for our gasoline because we won't let American oil companies here."[16]

To be fair, the Mexican government has taken steps over the years to liberalize other aspects of the economy. The North American Free Trade Agreement (NAFTA) tripled trade with the U.S. and Canada. Mexico's banking system is now one of the safest in Latin America, its currency is relatively stable, licensing procedures have been streamlined, the number of state-owned enterprises has been reduced, and many sectors of the economy have been open to foreign investment and increased competition.

But Mexico still has a long way to go.

Each year the *Wall Street Journal* and the Heritage Foundation publish an "Index of Economic Freedom," in which they rank every country in the world (based on various economic variables) as free, mostly free, mostly unfree, or repressed. In the latest edition, Mexico ranks sixty-third (tied with Cambodia!) out of 155 countries examined, putting it at the lower end of the "mostly free" category. Almost three-quarters of the countries in the North America and Europe category have a better rating than Mexico's.

Particularly troubling is the fact that the country, in the words of the *Wall Street Journal*, "still lacks a credible rule of law."[17] Judicial corruption is rampant and there is little faith among ordinary Mexicans that they will be dealt with fairly or that their hard work will pay off.

Some claim that the United States has to do more to help the Mexican economy by providing aid for building essential infrastructure, improving education, and the like. But no amount of outside aid will do any good if Mexico won't liberalize further and bring its underground economy out into the open. Privatizing Pemex would be a good place to start, but since the company's earnings represent the bulk of Mexico's tax base, that is unlikely.

One is tempted to tell the Mexicans: Look, your economic way of doing things is not working. You can't provide enough jobs for your people. Meanwhile, we are able to provide jobs for our people and a good number of yours. So why don't you open up your economy to try to make it more like ours? In a May 2005 speech to government and business leaders in Mexico City, our ambassador to Mexico, Tony Garza, came close, stating the obvious: "Let's be honest with each other. Reliance on remittances from the U.S. and windfall revenues from high oil prices is simply not an economic policy."[18]

As expected, members of the Mexican cabinet roundly condemned Garza, accusing him of—all together now—meddling in the internal affairs of Mexico. Meanwhile, some of the Mexican cabinet members doing the complaining do not just talk about meddling in America's internal affairs—they actually meddle in our internal affairs!

Creating economic prosperity is not the great mystery it used to be. The formula is pretty simple: keep taxes and regulations low, protect private property and enforce contracts, allow free trade, keep the money supply stable, ensure the free flow of capital, and educate your people.

As long as unemployed Mexicans have the option to "migrate" to the United States, the pressure is off the politicians in Mexico to make the necessary changes to fully open up their economy. Ironically, stopping the exodus of poor Mexicans actually might be to Mexico's benefit in the long run if it leads to real economic reform.

WHAT DOES MEXICO DO ABOUT ITS OWN ILLEGAL PROBLEM?

Since Mexico continually presses the U.S. to give its citizens more rights and opportunities in our country, I thought it might be instructive to examine how Mexico deals with its own illegal immigration problem. And believe it or not, illegal immigration is a large and growing problem in parts of Mexico, especially in areas along its southern border with Guatemala and Belize.

Author Luis Alberto Urrea described the current situation:

> Social services are swamped. Good jobs are going to illegals. Schools are overcrowded. The culture and the language are threatened. Crime is on the rise. I'm not talking about Phoenix, I'm talking about southern Mexico. It is hilarious to hear Mexican pols sounding like the Minutemen. But the numbers are higher as OTMs (Other Than Mexicans) augment the flow northward, swamping Mexico.[19]

Mexican officials consider the flow of aliens, mostly from Central America, a "security problem" and a headache for Mexico's border towns that have to put up with those who "get stuck [on their way to America] and they hang around the frontier cities making trouble, sleeping in the streets with no money."[20] In a six-part series tracing the journey of a seventeen-year-old illegal alien named Enrique from Honduras to North Carolina, the *Los Angeles Times* describes what happens when Enrique finds himself in southern Mexico:

> He is desperate for water. He spots a house. The people inside are not likely to give him any. Chiapas is fed up with Central American immigrants, says Hugo Angeles Cruz, a professor and migration expert at El Colegio de la Frontera Sur in Tapachula. They are poorer than Mexicans, and they are seen as backward and ignorant. People think they bring disease, prostitution, and crime and take away jobs. Some cannot be trusted. People in Chiapas talk of being robbed by migrants with guns and knives. They tell of an older woman who welcomed an immigrant into her home and was beaten to death with an iron pipe.
>
> Boys like Enrique are called "stinking undocumented." They are cursed, taunted. Dogs are set upon them. Barefoot children throw rocks at them. Some use slingshots. "Go to work." "Get out! Get out!"[21]

Still others excuse the aliens, in language you will recognize. Rodolfo Casillas, a migration expert at the Latin American School of Social Science in Mexico City, told the *Arizona Republic*: "They are coming and taking jobs the Mexicans don't want."[22]

I'm not making this up.

Indeed, big plantation owners say they prefer Guatemalans to Mexican workers because "Mexicans will not do the hard work of planting, cultivating, and picking."[23]

Sound familiar?

And just as in the United States, you have law enforcement trying to catch illegals while other Mexican agencies and human rights groups try to frustrate these efforts. All Mexico needs now is a group calling itself the "Minutohombres."

To combat Mexico's own illegal problem, Vicente Fox initiated "Operation Southern Plan" in 2001, which militarized Mexico's southern border to reduce the crime and corruption associated with alien smuggling and to round up and repatriate illegal aliens.

The tactics used by Mexican officials in the initial stages of Southern Plan go far beyond anything contemplated by even the most ardent anti–illegal immigration groups in the U.S. The army cordoned off certain areas and performed identity checks. According to one story, police "checked hotels, parks, bars, brothels, and other public places in search of illegal aliens."[24]

The plan has led to large increases in the number of deportations. The *Arizona Republic* reported: "The number of illegal immigrants detained in Mexico has risen nearly every year for the past decade, increasing 40 percent from 2000 to 2004. In 1997, authorities caught 86,973 illegal immigrants. By 2004, the number was 215,695. Of those, 211,218 were deported."[25]

However, the program has not been without controversy, and some of the complaints sound eerily familiar.

Human rights groups protest that the border is so militarized that aliens are forced to cross through remote, mountainous areas or use migrant smugglers. As a result, border deaths have increased. (In 2000, 136 aliens died crossing Mexico's southern border.)

These same groups also complain that illegal immigrants are too easily exploited. One UN official said illegal immigrants in Mexico are "highly vulnerable to human rights violations and become victims of degrading sexual exploitation and slavery-like practices, and are denied access to education and health care."[26]

Mexican scholar Rafael Fernandez de Castro claims Mexico's policy on its southern border is "more racist and discriminatory than that of the United States on [Mexico's] northern border."[27] (But then again, since our policy is neither racist nor discriminatory, it would have to be.)

What goes on along Mexico's southern border is of great importance to the United States. Because most of those crossing into southern Mexico are on their way here, our government rightly views Mexico's southern border as akin to a third U.S. border. Every OTM repatriated by Mexican authorities is one less we have to deal with here. By the same token, every OTM repatriated by Mexico is one less worker in competition with a Mexican citizen, either in Mexico or in the U.S.

The adage "follow the money" is not lost on the Mexican government. Remittances to Central America from the United States total about $10 billion annually. I'll bet that's money the Mexican government would prefer found its way to Mexico instead. So cutting off the flow of illegals from Central America through Mexico to the U.S. isn't just good politics, it's good business, too.

Make no mistake: Mexico's newfound respect for the sanctity of international borders extends only to its own southern border, and it has much less to do with our security than with Mexico's desire to be the exclusive supplier of cheap labor to the U.S.

WHAT SHOULD OUR MEXICO POLICY BE?

If Mexico continues to actively undermine our laws, then we should take steps to penalize our belligerent neighbor. Specifically, we should respond in a way the Mexican government will understand, first by expelling Mexican diplomats who interfere in the internal affairs of our country. In 2002 Mexico petulantly expelled a dozen American college students for domestic interference because they engaged in a protest while legally in the country. We should likewise expel Mexican consuls who regularly lobby local governments, organize protests, hire lawyers for illegal aliens, or try to corrupt our educational system.

Additionally, we should eliminate *legal* immigration from Mexico until Congress certifies that our neighbor is acting in good faith to prevent illegal border crossings.

Fox once said of the San Diego border fence that it "must be demolished." "No country that is proud of itself should construct walls... it doesn't make any sense," he lectured.[28]

Words fail me here... almost.

No country that is proud of itself should stand by as its people escape in droves, much less encourage them to do so, because its leaders cannot provide them with jobs or a decent life and then scold as ungrateful the country that does. A recent poll by the Pew Hispanic Center found that 46 percent of Mexicans would go live in the United States if they had the means and opportunity, and that 21 percent would do so illegally.[29] These results prompted a *Christian Science Monitor* editorial that asked, "Is Mexico still a nation?"[30] Mexico is in no position to lecture us about pride.

Mexico is not the aggrieved party in this situation—the United States is. Mexico is the *belligerent*. It is the sovereignty of our country that is under assault and it is exclusively for us to decide how best to respond.

It is not in our power nor should it be our intention to dictate how Mexico should arrange its economic and governmental affairs. But it seems to me that the Mexican government has an obligation to its people to change and the Mexican people have an obligation to their country to make sure the government changes. By continually looking the other way on illegal immigration, the U.S. has essentially become an enabler of Mexico's corruption and economic foolishness. It is long past time we stopped.

In the wake of the 2004 elections, countless Hollywood leftists, college professors, and other cultural elitists told us that they just could not bear to live any longer in a country headed by George W. Bush. They were going to prove their moral superiority by leaving the country for more progressive regimes. Some said they would go to Europe, but the vast majority said they would head off to Canada. Not a single one said, "I've had it. I can't live in red America another day. I'm off to Mexico!"

Even with its obvious climatic advantages over our northern neighbor, no one was willing to go quite that far, for obvious reasons. Maybe when our left-wing sore losers begin considering Mexico as a destination after another electoral pasting, we will be able to say that Mexico has turned a corner. It cannot come a moment too soon.

CHAPTER SIX

IS AMERICA COMPLICIT IN ILLEGAL IMMIGRATION?

"With no penalty for hiring an illegal alien being imposed, there is simply no reason to obey the law. This whole policy of non-enforcement has created a state of anarchy. No longer do greedy employers have to obey tax, insurance, or Social Security laws."

> —Matthew James Reindl, small business owner testifying before Congress

FOR ALL THAT **M**EXICO DOES to encourage illegal aliens to come to the United States, our own government has done as much and probably more. You can't really blame the millions of illegals already here and the hundreds of thousands who join them every year. They are, for the most part, responding to a demand for cheap, unskilled, and unregulated labor by American businesses and individuals. They are also responding to the unwillingness of successive presidents, congresses, governors, state legislatures, and especially local officials to enforce our immigration laws.

It's never been the case that we *can't* control illegal immigration—it's that we *won't*. Instead of making the effort, we make excuses. Speaking in December 2003 of the crisis on our borders, former Homeland Security secretary Tom Ridge said: "The bottom line is, as a country we have to come to grips with the presence of eight to twelve million illegals, afford them some kind of legal status some way, but also as a country decide what our immigration policy is and then enforce it."[1]

We hear this argument a lot. But haven't we *already* decided what our immigration policy should be? Isn't that why we have all those immigration laws on the books? Why not try enforcing those for a change?

But the negligence goes far beyond not enforcing our laws. While the Border Patrol is fighting a heroic battle against insurmountable odds, the rest of the government either turns a blind eye or actually works to make it easier for illegal aliens to settle into American life. A few examples:

- If an employer submits to the Social Security Administration (SSA) a fraudulent Social Security number being used by an illegal alien, the SSA is barred by federal law from sharing that information with immigration authorities at the Department of Homeland Security.
- Even as the death toll from illegal immigration mounts, cities from coast to coast have passed so-called "sanctuary" laws that forbid local police from cooperating with federal immigration officials or even asking anyone whether they are legally in the United States.
- Throughout the country, states are offering illegal aliens all sorts of benefits, including driver's licenses, in-state tuition for colleges, and adult education.
- The law against hiring illegal aliens has never been vigorously enforced, and since September 11, enforcement has been practically nonexistent. The focus now is on nabbing terrorists and securing critical infrastructure deemed vital to national security. For instance, Operation Tarmac resulted in the arrest of more than 1,000 illegals working in *secure* areas of domestic airports. The result? The Government Accountability Office found that in 2004 the Immigration and Customs Enforcement agency brought just three actions against companies for hiring illegals.
- Under a program called Basic Pilot, employees can phone an 800 number to find out if a potential hire's Social Security number is legitimate. Sounds great, right? Well, not so great. The program is *voluntary*. As *Time* magazine noted, "Imagine what compliance with tax laws would be if filing a 1040 were optional."[2]

Would-be illegal immigrants get the message loud and clear. It translates easily into Spanish for those Mexicans and Central Americans who want to come north for economic opportunity. It translates just as easily into the language of the Islamofascists who want to come here to kill Americans. The message is this: cross our porous borders and you are home free—welcome to America. Oh, and please don't kill us.

THE WELCOME MAT

Vladimir Lenin once said that capitalists would sell their enemies the rope with which to hang them, but I think even he would be surprised at how brazen American businesses are in catering to illegals. The July 18, 2005, cover story of *BusinessWeek* magazine, titled "Embracing Illegals," is a shocking exposé of the extent to which American companies put profits before the good of their country. The greed creed is epitomized by John Wise, chief executive of Viscom International, which sells prepaid phone cards: "The guy that just got here is going to make a lot more calls than the guy who has been here three generations; it doesn't matter if they're legal or not."[3]

That's the spirit, John! As long as you make a buck, who cares? And it's not just the big companies that cater to illegal aliens. Even illegal aliens who cannot obtain a driver's license can still buy cars. As one used-car saleman in California told National Public Radio, "I know they're illegal. I don't ask them. I really don't care.... Money is green, that's what everybody wants, you know?"[4]

Much of the problem stems from a 2001 Treasury Department decision allowing banks to accept the matrícula consular card as a legitimate form of identification. The card is issued by the Mexican government to, well, just about anyone who can complete the application. Matrículas are available at any Mexican consulate in the United States for about $30. All an applicant needs to get a card is a Mexican birth certificate—real or fake.

How widespread is the use of the card? One illegal family cited in the *BusinessWeek* article used the matrícula to get a car loan from a local dealer, cell-phone service from Verizon Communications, and a bank account from Wells Fargo. Others have used the card to obtain health insurance. Blue Cross of California and BlueCross BlueShield of Georgia say they are "helping to mitigate the health insurance crisis" by offering insurance to matrícula holders. Says a Blue Cross of California spokesman: "It's a health care issue, not an immigration issue."[5]

The matrículas have worked so well for Mexican illegals that the governments of Guatemala, Ecuador, and Brazil issue their own versions of the cards. El Salvador, Colombia, Argentina, Honduras, Peru, and Poland are considering them too.

Wells Fargo "pioneered" acceptance of the matrícula after the *police department* in Austin, Texas (a sanctuary city), asked banks for help in preventing holdups of illegals who "tend to carry wads of cash."[6] Al Montoya, senior vice president in charge of growth markets for Wells Fargo, told the *Arizona Republic*, "We have no reason to ask a person's residency status. Any business decision is based on value and what's going to provide shareholder value."[7] Translation: we don't care as long as we make a buck.

Meanwhile, as a way to attract Hispanic customers, Bank of America has launched a program (called SafeSend) that lets Hispanics transfer money to Mexico... for free. The bank's Liam McGee explains: "We are proud to help millions of Hispanics send money for free to loved ones in Mexico. Adding the free SafeSend feature to our checking accounts is our way of saying that we want to do much more—we want to be their bank of choice and help Hispanics develop rewarding, long-term financial relationships."[8]

So much for being good corporate citizens. It reminds me of a scene in an episode of *Law & Order*. The Lennie character, played by the late Jerry Orbach, is running down some information on a murder. He calls the victim's bank to ask some questions and is shocked by what he hears. He puts down the phone and says to his partner, "Can you believe it? The bank didn't even check to see if his Social Security number was real!" Hey, Lennie, get with it! Banks don't care if the Social Security number is real or if the customer is illegal. All that matters is whether the deal "provides shareholder value."

Take the case of Javier and Janet, an illegal couple in Arizona. According to the *Arizona Republic:*

> They used fake Social Security numbers to land their jobs. To be able to file tax returns, they obtained real individual tax identification numbers.... They got a mortgage with an 8.5 percent interest rate with credit they had built up over the years making purchases on credit cards obtained with their fake Social Security numbers.[9]

In typical politically correct fashion, the article was headlined "Undocumented immigrant family embraces middle-class America." Do they sound "undocumented" to you? And since when is middle-class America built on document fraud?

These policies make amnesty for illegal aliens a virtual fait accompli. According to *BusinessWeek:* "Companies are taking a position similar to the president's, in effect saying: there's no point in pretending that millions of people aren't here, so let's find a way to deal with them."[10]

Make that: let's find a way to profit from them while wages continue to decline, schools continue to fail, hospitals continue to close, and society continues to fragment.

By giving the matrícula consular card its imprimatur, the Treasury Department has allowed business to profit at the expense of our national interest. This monumentally stupid and unilateral decision, which was never approved by Congress, must be reversed.

If businesses aren't targeting illegal aliens as consumers, they are hiring them as workers. So it should come as no surprise that pro-business groups are right in the thick of efforts to promote illegal alien amnesty. One such group, Americans for Border and Economic Security, is charging business and other interests between $50,000 and $250,000 to join. They plan a massive political-style campaign to convince you that immigration is a good thing for America—except that when they say "immigration," they really mean "illegal immigration."

The "economic security" component of the group's agenda is a guest worker/amnesty plan for illegal aliens that will provide an ongoing source of cheap labor. These business interests want us to believe, as *National Review* cleverly put it, "that our vast twenty-first-century economy can't function without a constant flow of high-school dropouts from overseas."[11] It is absurd.

As for the "border security" part, it is mere window dressing. According to the *Los Angeles Times*, it is nothing but "an attempt to mollify a vocal bloc of cultural conservatives...who argue that undocumented workers [illegal aliens to you and me] present a security threat and take some jobs that could be filled by Americans."[12] I don't know about you, but I'm in no mood to be mollified; I'm in a mood to do battle with the special interests perpetrating this fraud.

THE 1986 AMNESTY

How did we get into this mess? We asked for it when we enacted the Immigration Reform and Control Act (IRCA) of 1986—one of the most misnamed bills in history, since it did not reform or control anything. Indeed, you would be hard-pressed to find any piece of legislation in the history of our country that failed as miserably as IRCA. (The act is sometimes also referred to as Simpson-Mazzoli, after the Senate and House sponsors, Republican Alan Simpson of Wyoming and Democrat Romano Mazzoli of Kentucky.) The act did nothing its advocates—or even some of its opponents—said it would; in fact, in almost every case the opposite happened.

The bill was supposed to be a grand compromise, giving liberals and conservatives some of what each side wanted. Both sides should have known better. As Eugene McCarthy once cautioned, "Remember that the worst accidents occur in or near the middle of the road." This was an accident of monumental proportions.

IRCA offered a tempting bargain—amnesty for illegal aliens in the country since 1982 in exchange for putting into law, for the first time ever, penalties for employers who hired illegals, with the promise of strict enforcement. Almost twenty years and millions of illegals later, it is hard to imagine that the most controversial part of this plan was not the amnesty, but the employer sanctions!

Like many of the current illegal immigration proposals, the amnesty portion was meant to recognize the "facts on the ground." The argument was as simple as it was simple-minded. Illegal immigrants who had been living in the United States for a long period of time would be difficult to find, and even if we could find them, deporting them would disrupt our economy and betray our immigrant heritage.

The major provision on employer sanctions was intended to close a gaping loophole in U.S. law, the so-called Texas Proviso of 1952, which made it unlawful for illegals to take a job in the United States *but did not make it against the law for U.S. employers to hire them.* In other words, up until the time of IRCA, it was the illegal alien, not the employer, who took all the risk. Simpson-Mazzoli was supposed to change that.

President Ronald Reagan recognized the importance of employer sanctions at the signing ceremony, saying, "The employer sanctions program is the keystone and major element. It will remove the incentive for illegal immigration by eliminating the job opportunities which draw illegal aliens here."[13]

But there was also a third, highly controversial provision. It provided that illegals who worked in agriculture for ninety days during the previous year would be made temporary residents, and if they put in ninety days each year during the preceding three years—or got someone to say they did—their status would change from temporary to permanent.

Got that? Illegals who worked just ninety days a year for the three years prior to passage of IRCA were put in front of the estimated 1.9 million people around the world who at that time were waiting, some as long as twelve years, to get into the country legally. These ninety-day workers were known as Special Agricultural Workers (SAWs). Special indeed!

Experience over the last twenty years suggests that this was perhaps the most inane provision in the entire bill, and that is saying something. Liberals in Congress even insisted that these Special *Agricultural* Workers not be limited to farm work!

Looking back on some of the predictions made during the lengthy debate on the 1986 amnesty bill, it is amazing how so many were so sure about so much that was so wrong. But it is important that we see just how wrong almost everyone was so that we don't make the same mistakes again. Here are some examples.

Democratic congressman Robert Garcia of New York was a strong opponent of the bill. He thought the amnesty provisions were far too onerous (no joke) and claimed that "a liberal estimate of the number of people that would have been admitted under the legalization program in Simpson-Mazzoli is perhaps 25 percent."[14] The actual number was more like 60 percent.

Senator Ted Kennedy strongly opposed IRCA, fretting that the employer sanctions would discourage employers from hiring Hispanic workers. He called the sanctions "an unwarranted badge of discrimination against millions of law-abiding, hard-working American citizens of Hispanic descent."[15]

Far-left congressman Don Edwards of California likewise declared employer sanctions "an invitation to racial discrimination."[16]

Then there was Lawrence H. Fuchs, the executive director of the Select Commission on Immigration and Refugee Policy and a strong IRCA supporter. Writing in the *New York Times,* Fuchs confidently predicted:

> Nor will [IRCA] open the floodgates to immigration. Even the most dramatic forecasts do not predict more than two million will apply for legalization. Overall, the Simpson-Mazzoli bill will affect only marginally the total number of immigrants lawfully admitted in the years ahead.... And it will take seven to ten years to develop a universally secure system to validate those who can work and who can't. But by that time, the incentive to enter the country illegally will have been removed.[17]

Twenty years later, and we're still waiting.

Even the brilliant Daniel Patrick Moynihan was taken in, arguing in support of the bill that "employers will not hire any illegal aliens, even those who have resided and worked here for many years, if they face penalties for doing so."[18]

Republican senator Phil Gramm of Texas said IRCA "holds out great peril, peril that employers dealing in good faith could be subject to criminal penalties and in fact go to jail for making a mistake in hiring an illegal alien."[19]

Senator Dennis DeConcini, a Democrat from Arizona, proclaimed, "If we make it illegal to hire an illegal alien, employers will simply not hire illegal aliens."[20]

Democrat Charles Schumer, at the time a New York congressman and the author of the controversial SAW provision, confidently stated in a *New York Times* op-ed, "It is agreed that employer sanctions would probably be effective." He went on to make a series of assertions that would embarrass, if not humiliate, a person of lesser self-esteem:

> One of the problems with interest-group lobbyists is that they inevitably draw attention to the flaws in a proposal. How can we be sure that employer sanctions would be enforced or that illegal aliens won't forge identity cards? What makes us certain that those already in the country will take advantage of the amnesty offered them? These questions are valid, but they miss the point; a law even with these flaws would be greatly preferable to the present situation.[21]

Can't you just feel Chuck's pain? The nerve of those "interests" asking such pesky questions! What makes them even peskier is that we now know that the questioners were right and Schumer was wrong. One thing is clear: the illegal immigration problem post-IRCA is not "greatly preferable" to what it was in 1986. It is actually much, much worse.

WHY POLITICIANS SHOULDN'T MAKE PREDICTIONS

Now that we have read all the self-assured predictions about what would happen following enactment of the 1986 amnesty, let's take a look at what actually happened.

1986 PREDICTION: Illegal immigration will slow and
eventually stop.

REALITY: In the immediate aftermath of the 1986 amnesty, illegal immigration did fall, as potential crossers waited to see if
the promised enforcement would materialize. It never did, and
the second "amnesty wave" of illegals began...and continues
to this day.

1986 PREDICTION: Businesses will not hire illegal aliens
for fear of being fined.

REALITY: Written into the 1986 law was a loophole so big millions of illegal workers snuck through it. The law states that
for employers to be fined, they have to knowingly hire an illegal alien. Employers taken in by a phony Social Security card
cannot be penalized if they obey a few simple rules or ask a
few simple questions. No wonder employers keep hiring illegal
aliens with impunity.

1986 PREDICTION: Only a small percentage of illegal
aliens will take advantage of the amnesty.

REALITY: The total number of illegal aliens applying for
amnesty was so large it stunned and overwhelmed federal officials, who simply could not keep up with applications despite
opening 109 offices nationwide to handle the load.

1986 PREDICTION: The total number of immigrants lawfully
admitted in the years ahead will increase only marginally.

REALITY: IRCA unleashed a "chain migration" that has allowed
one country, Mexico, to dominate legal immigration. Here's
how it works. An immigrant brings his wife, who brings her
sister, who brings her husband, who brings...you get the
point. This "echo effect" is why Mexico will continue to grab
the lion's share of legal immigration slots for years to come, to
the detriment of our melting pot heritage.

1986 PREDICTION: The number of those applying for legal residency as Special Agricultural Workers will be small.

REALITY: The actual number was three times greater than expected, largely because of fraud. Sometimes the fraud was downright comical, as when applicants qualified who didn't know that strawberries don't grow on trees. In another bizarre instance, a woman in New Jersey with a five-acre garden plot certified that more than 1,000 illegal aliens had worked her land. One American official in Mexico City admitted the obvious: "This program is uniquely vulnerable to fraud."[22] I'll say.

Less amusing is how Mohammed Abouhalima—a New York cabbie who never worked on an American farm—gained legal status under the SAW program by claiming he picked beans in Florida. Abouhalima elected to forego the farm life, instead using his new legal status for foreign travel (to Afghanistan) and worker training (to become a terrorist). He went on to play a leading role in the 1993 World Trade Center bombing.

Despite all the wrongheaded predictions, there was one group that got it right. Scholars at several Mexican think tanks predicted that the new provisions would not reduce the number of Mexicans crossing the border annually because of Mexico's unemployment and high U.S. wages. Gerardo Bueno, a demographer at the nation's leading think tank, Colegio de Mexico, told the *Phoenix Gazette* that the law would "not necessarily be a disincentive for illegal workers nor for U.S. employers."[23] The man has a knack for understatement!

The 1986 bill promised to deliver amnesty for illegal aliens and strict enforcement of immigration laws going forward. The illegal aliens and the business lobby got their amnesty. But here we are—two decades later and apparently none the wiser—still waiting for the promised strict enforcement that hasn't come. And now the same groups who sold us a bill of goods in 1986 have come back asking us for another amnesty, with the same promises of strict enforcement. It would be idiotic to listen to them again.

THE ENFORCEMENT EXPERIENCE

What is most disturbing is the willingness of open-borders advocates to ignore our successful experience with enforcement. A few
examples:

- In 2002, the Social Security Administration (SSA) sent out
  almost a million "no match" letters to employers who filed
  W-2s with information that did not match SSA records. In
  some cases the cause was simply a typo or misspelling, but in
  most cases illegals were lying to their employers and many
  lost their jobs. Soon, however, business interests and identity-
  group grievance-mongers organized to put an end to the program. As a result, there has been a 90 percent reduction in
  such letters.
- In 1998 about fifty INS agents raided Vidalia onion farms in
  Georgia to catch illegal field hands. The program, Operation
  Southern Denial, was successful—too successful. As word of
  the raids spread, illegals stopped showing up for work, upset-
  ting farmers who have only a four- to six-week window to
  pick their crops. Soon the Georgia congressional delegation
  was involved, demanding that the INS back off. The result
  was an unprecedented "mini-amnesty" just for illegals working to pick this crop.
- Stung by the reaction to the Vidalia onion raid, enforcement
  officials tried a different approach with Nebraska's meat-
  packing industry, dubbed Operation Vanguard. Instead of
  raids, the INS subpoenaed the hiring records of packing-
  houses and compared them with data from the SSA. Dis-
  crepancies were found in almost 20 percent of the work
  force. When word got out that the feds were serious, illegal
  workers headed for the hills. However, as in Georgia, the INS
  was forced to back off after pressure from Nebraska's congressional delegation, the meatpackers, farmers, and Hispanic groups.

- After September 11, immigration authorities conducted a "Special Registration" program for visitors from Islamic countries. When it became clear the government meant business, thousands of illegals, mostly Pakistanis, left. According to the *Washington Post*:

> Of the 120,000 or so Pakistanis who lived near here, 15,000, maybe more, have left for Canada, Europe, or Pakistan, according to Pakistani government estimates. The departures began after September 11, 2001, when federal agents began stopping and detaining hundreds of Pakistanis. The exodus accelerated five months ago, when the Department of Homeland Security required that every male Pakistani visa holder age sixteen or older register with the Bureau of Immigration and Customs Enforcement.[24]

So now you know the dirty little secret that the open-borders fanatics hoped you wouldn't discover: enforcement works—but only if the government has the stomach to see it through.

CHAPTER SEVEN

THE LEFT AND RIGHT ARE WRONG

"Despite the fact that [Cesar] Chavez is these days revered among Mexican American activists, the labor leader in his day was no more tolerant of illegal immigration than the Arizona Minutemen are now."

—Ruben Navarette

SUPPORT FOR ILLEGAL IMMIGRATION is one of those rare causes in which elements on the Left and the Right have found common ground, albeit for entirely different reasons. Demetrios Papademetriou of the pro–illegal immigrant Migration Policy Institute probably summed it up best: "The Left doesn't mind, or probably loves, beating up on employers, but he wants to hold illegal immigrants safe. The Right, they don't like illegal immigrants, but they don't want to make it difficult for employers to do what they think they have to do."[1]

It's a match made in...never mind.

But while the Left is just somewhat splintered on the issue, the disagreement on the Right is downright fractious. In the December 31, 2004, issue of *National Review*, former White House speechwriter David Frum issued this warning to the Republican Party:

No issue, not one, threatens to do more damage to the Republican coalition than immigration. There's no issue where the beliefs and interests of the party rank-and-file diverge more radically from the beliefs and interests of the party's leaders. Immigration for Republicans in 2005 is what crime was for Democrats in 1965 or abortion in 1975: a vulnerable point at which a strong-minded opponent could drive a wedge that would shatter the GOP.[2]

Frum is exactly right. Before long, Rush Limbaugh, Sean Hannity, Laura Ingraham, and others were hammering the same theme. Sad to say, the divide is as wide and deep as ever and shows no signs of closing, which is one of the reasons I decided to write this book. What makes it even worse is that some of those who excuse or even celebrate illegal immigration are otherwise some of conservatism's stars. Which brings us to...

THE STRANGE CASE OF
THE *WALL STREET JOURNAL*

The *Wall Street Journal* editorial page is a must-read for conservatives every day. But on the issue of illegal immigration, the *Journal* is conservatism's crazy old aunt in the attic.

The *Journal*'s idiosyncratic—some might say idiotic—position on illegal immigration can be summed up in five little words: "there shall be open borders."

Famously (or infamously, depending on your point of view), on July 3, 1984, the *Journal* ran an editorial titled "In Praise of Huddled Masses," stating:

> If Washington still wants to "do something" about immigration, we propose a five-word constitutional amendment: there shall be open borders. Perhaps this policy is overly ambitious in today's world, but the U.S. became the world's envy by trumpeting precisely this kind of heresy. Our greatest heresy is that we believe in people as the great resource of our land. Those who would live in freedom have voted over the centuries with their feet. Wherever the state abused its people, beginning with the Puritan pilgrims and continuing today in places like Ho Chi Minh City and Managua, they've aimed for our shores. They—we—have astonished the world with the country's success.[3]

The prevailing sentiment at the *Journal* seems to be: "Borders? *Borders?* We don't need no stinkin' borders!"

The latest such editorial was by the late, great *Journal* editorial page editor Robert Bartley, who wrote on July 2, 2001, a mere eight weeks before the most devastating attack ever on our homeland:

> Reformist Mexican president Vicente Fox raises eyebrows with his suggestion that over a decade or two NAFTA should evolve into something like the European Union, with open borders for not only goods and investment but also people. He can rest assured that there is one voice north of the Rio Grande that supports his vision. To wit, this newspaper.[4]

Suffice it to say that there has not been a single open-borders editorial by the *Journal* since September 11. Had the carnage wrought by terrorists taking advantage of our lax immigration enforcement perhaps caused the *Journal* to finally come around on the issue or at least entertain second thoughts? I doubt it.

Most likely the editors understand that if they renewed their call for open borders after what happened right outside their office windows in lower Manhattan on a beautiful September day, they would look completely ridiculous, out of touch with reality, and ready for relocation to Bellevue.

Since September 11 the *Journal* has had to find new ways to sell its "open borders" nonsense to a public that overwhelmingly wants the government to get tough on illegal immigration. Its latest line is that we have tried mightily to control our borders, but it hasn't worked. In one editorial the *Journal* declared, "Despite nearly twenty years of efforts to 'crack down on the borders,' the immigrants keep coming."[5] This is from another:

> The number of border patrol agents tripled and the most popular corridors for illegals—San Diego and El Paso—were sealed off. The thinking was that the treacherous mountains and deserts in between

would serve as natural deterrents. But once again, the border brigades were wrong....As one government official told us, "We underestimated the will of these people."[6]

Sealing off favored crossing points while leaving unprotected large swaths of our border where there is rough terrain is what passes for a "crackdown" in the precincts of the *Journal*, but I can tell you such a claim would elicit guffaws in Arizona or the other border states that are being overrun. The *Journal's* claim would likewise come as a shock to the millions of illegals that have streamed unmolested across our border.

It is amazing that while *Journal* editors have never doubted our ability to bring democracy to war-torn Iraq (a notion I share), when it comes to controlling *our own* borders they don't think we can handle it.

I wish we had been cracking down on the border for twenty years. Had we, things today would be quite different. As the *Journal* itself has unwittingly admitted, the enforcement efforts on the border in San Diego and El Paso are so successful that illegals don't try to cross there anymore. We can replicate that success all along our southern border—but only if our will exceeds that of the smugglers.

WITH FRIENDS LIKE THESE...

In one particularly vituperative editorial, Jason Riley, the *Journal's* senior editorial page writer, spat: "So determined is conservatism's nativist wing [to control illegal immigration] that it's even made common cause with radical environmentalists and zero-population-growth fanatics on the leftist fringe."[7]

Oh dear! Do you feel yourself going weak in the knees? Neither do I.

Instead of the "nativist wing," he might have called us the "wing that believes in enforcing the law." And in fact, when it comes to immigration, it is the "open borders" *Journal* that has thrown in with left-wing crackpots, anti-Americans, and racists. You want fringe? Let's start with these:

- The Mexican American Legal Defense and Education Fund (MALDEF), whose co-founder Mario Obledo once warned, "California is going to be a Hispanic state, and anyone who doesn't like it should leave. They should go back to Europe."[8] That's a strange thing to say about a state with 4.8 million Asian Americans and 2.2 million African Americans.
- The Movimiento Estudiantil Chicano de Aztlán (MEChA), whose constitution calls for the "liberation" of Aztlán (although we are assured it's only a "spiritual" liberation).[9]
- The American Immigration Lawyers Association, whose executive director, Jeanne Butterfield, once ran the Palestine Solidarity Committee, the political arm of the Popular Front for the Liberation of Palestine terror group.
- The National Immigration Forum, which signed a November 2001 document characterizing the September 11 attacks as a "crime" rather than an act of war and has received funding from George Soros's Open Society Institute.
- The ACLU's Immigration Rights Project, which filed amicus curiae briefs in support of "dirty bomb" suspect Jose Padilla.
- The National Council of La Raza (la raza means "the race" in Spanish), whose spokeswoman said in the wake of September 11, "There's no relationship between immigration and terrorism."[10] The 9-11 Commission, of course, begs to differ.

I'll forgo untangling the web between these groups and other anti-American and even some pro-Communist elements (Laura Ingraham does an excellent job in her terrific book *Shut Up and Sing*). All you really need to know is that these groups—along with the *Wall Street Journal*—are working toward the same goal: open borders.

Not all is lost, however. On Lou Dobbs's television show, viewer Fernando Peña of San Jose, California, nails it: "As a Latino, I am sickened by groups such as MEChA and MALDEF. These are racist, anti-American groups."[11]

To the *Wall Street Journal*, however, these very same groups represent Ronald Reagan's "shining city on a hill." Go figure.

IS THE STATUS QUO AMNESTY?

Congressman Jeff Flake and Senator Ted Kennedy agree on next to nothing. Flake is one of the most conservative members of the House of Representatives while Kennedy is one of the Senate's biggest liberals. However, when it comes to illegal immigration, they have more in common than not.

Together they push one of the more bizarre arguments you will hear from the guest-worker crowd, namely that the status quo is amnesty. How, you ask, can that possibly be? Well, let's hear directly from the liberal member of this odd couple.

Here is what Ted Kennedy said in a statement on the Senate floor the day he introduced his guest worker/amnesty bill: "If there's any amnesty involved, it's what [illegal aliens] have today—an acquiescence in their presence, because countless businesses could not function without them since no American workers can be found to fill their jobs."[12]

It should be pointed out that in 1986 Kennedy predicted that to avoid employer sanctions businesses would simply not hire Hispanics. Now he tells us these very same businesses would not be able to function without the Hispanics they have hired. If love is never having to say you're sorry, liberalism is never having to admit you were wrong.

In any event, the argument that the status quo is akin to amnesty is inconsistent with the odd couple's own rhetoric. I'll let Kennedy make my point for me. In the very same speech cited above, in which he equates the status quo to amnesty, he also said: "...millions of today's immigrant workers are not here legally. They and their families live shadow lives in constant fear of deportation, and are easy targets for abuse and exploitation by unscrupulous employers and criminals as well."[13]

If Kennedy truly believes what I've just quoted, how can he possibly call it amnesty? Does it sound like amnesty to you?

Kennedy and Flake are fully aware that admitting their plan is amnesty would doom it. So they tie themselves in rhetorical knots to convince us otherwise. But the "status quo is amnesty" argument insults our intelligence. When you break it down it becomes even more absurd. Here is its crux: what illegal aliens enjoy now is a form of amnesty; we are going to give them something even better, but don't you dare call it amnesty!

Logic like that can make your head hurt.

Finally, if you really believe that the status quo is amnesty, let me ask you this: if you were an illegal alien, which would you choose, the status quo or some form of legalization? Kennedy and Flake may believe their rhetoric, but I doubt you'd find a single illegal alien who would.

LETTUCE LIBERALS

Another obsession among the open-borders crowd is what will happen to the price of lettuce if we stop illegal immigration. It permeates the debate. You pick up the paper and see things like this over a letter to the editor, "Would you pay $8 for lettuce?"[14] Or this quote from a farmer hooked on illegal labor, "If they think $3 gas is bad, imagine $20 for a head of lettuce, or a $5 peach."[15]

You've heard of limousine liberals? I call these folks lettuce liberals. You can be conservative 99 percent of the time and still be a lettuce liberal. At a meeting in the Capitol with several members of the Arizona congressional delegation and Arizona governor Janet Napolitano, one of my guts-up conservative colleagues made the case for a guest-worker program. Without it, he asked, "What's going to happen to the price of lettuce?"

Al Qaeda is looking to ship a nuke across our southern border and we're supposed to wring our hands over the price of lettuce? Not this congressman.

Besides, it is unlikely that the price of lettuce will ever go the way of a barrel of crude oil. Despite all the dire predictions of lettuce at a billion dollars a head, the evidence suggests that its price would rise very little in the absence of illegal labor.

To date, the definitive study on the price of agricultural products and illegal labor is "How Much Is That Tomato in the Window?" (*Tomato*?

They must not have gotten the memo!) by Wallace Huffman and Alan McCunn of Iowa State University. Their 1996 study concluded that in the absence of illegal labor, wages for workers would rise about 30 percent in the short term and 15 percent over the long term. But because the price of labor is just one of many important factors, the impact on prices would be negligible.

This mirrors the results of similar studies. In 1995 agricultural economist Philip Martin of the University of California–Davis found that labor accounts for only about 10 percent of the price of a head of lettuce at the retail level. He concluded that even if pickers' wages doubled consumers would notice little effect.

More recently, in 2002, Martin did another study, "How We Eat: 2002, Obesity," that again examined this issue. According to the U.S. Bureau of Labor Statistics data cited in his report, the 112 million "consumer units" (that's you and me) in the U.S. spent an average of $353 each on fruits and vegetables in 2002. Farmers got about 16 percent of that amount, or $61. Of that amount, about $20 went to farm workers. In a nutshell, that means for every dollar consumers spend on lettuce, about five cents goes to farm workers.

Suppose farm labor costs were to increase 40 percent in the absence of illegal workers? Martin explains: "[T]otal spending on fruits and vegetables would rise by $8, from $353 a year to $361 a year. However, for a typical seasonal farm worker, earnings could rise to $11,200 a year, up from $8,000."[16]

The lettuce liberals are willing to overlook the billions of dollars illegal immigrants cost our economy, the crime, the balkanization, and the potential national security threat so they won't have to pay a measly *eight dollars a year* more for fruits and vegetables? Talk about selling out.

Well, you say, increasing wages by 40 percent still might not be enough to attract American workers to field jobs. What happens then? Farmers would do what they have always done: adapt. Necessity, after all, is the mother of invention. As Martin says, "wage increases may lead to farm productivity improvements, so that consumer prices may decrease rather than increase." Indeed, it could very well be that availability of such a large pool of unskilled and low-cost labor actually impedes economic progress.

In an op-ed in the *Washington Post*, the Center for Immigration Studies' Mark Krikorian illustrates the point:

> In the early 1960s, during the hearings that led to the termination of the bracero program because of exploitation of Mexican workers, a spokesman for tomato farmers claimed that "the use of braceros [imported laborers] is absolutely essential to the survival of the tomato industry." Congress went ahead and discontinued the program. Without the cheap Mexican labor, farmers increasingly mechanized the harvest over the next three decades, resulting in a quadrupling in the production of tomatoes destined for processing—and a fall in real prices.[17]

The other option is that farmers will plant different, less labor-intensive crops that have higher value and bigger profit margins and leave lettuce and the like to farmers abroad. Either way, the end result will be the same: as much lettuce as you can eat at a price you are willing to pay.

Today, depending on where you live, a head of lettuce costs about $1.80. Without illegal immigration it would at most be about a dime more, and probably closer to a nickel. If the extra nickel bugs you that much, think of it as a nickel for national security.

Lettuce liberals, however, have expanded their field, seeing price increases everywhere without illegal labor. In an article titled "Imagining America without illegal immigrants," the *New York Times* claimed:

> Without [cheap illegal labor], fruit and vegetables would rot in fields. Toddlers in Manhattan would be without nannies. Towels at hotels in states like Florida, Texas, and California would go unlaundered. Commuters at airports from Miami to Newark would be stranded as taxi cabs sat driverless. Home improvement projects across the Sun Belt would grind to a halt. And bedpans and lunch trays at nursing homes in Chicago, New York, Houston, and Los Angeles would go uncollected.[18]

Would there be some dislocation if all illegal immigrants went home? Probably. Would it last long? Probably not. There are large parts of the country that are relatively untouched by illegal labor. And believe it or not, in those places the fast-food restaurants, hotels, and farms all seem to do just fine, thank you.

If the illegal labor spigot were cut off, those parts of the country hooked on illegal labor—places like California, Texas, Illinois, and Florida—would have to compete for workers from other parts of the country. Such competition would be good for workers. As George Borjas noted, "The workers would be slightly wealthier, and the employers would be slightly poorer, but everything would get done."

Our liberal elites like to claim they're the champions of the working class, but their real attitude is "Give us cheap illegal labor for our privileged lifestyle; Americans need not apply."

THE PROBLEM WILL SOLVE ITSELF

One of the more curious arguments we're starting to hear more and more came from Matt Dowd, chief strategist for the Bush-Cheney 2004 campaign. In a column for the *New York Times,* Dowd says that the issue of illegal immigration from Mexico is "resolving itself." He writes:

> The aging of the population in Mexico coupled with Mexico's economic expansion mean that jobs in Mexico will be more plentiful, thereby prompting fewer young people to come to the United States in search of work.... If the trend continues, it could be that we've already seen the high-water mark of illegal Mexican immigration.[19]

Dowd's analysis sounds so reasonable you almost want to wipe your brow, give a big "whew," and move on to another book. Except that, like so much else in this debate, we've heard it all before.

Demographers have long been predicting that Mexico's sustained job creation and lower birth rate would cause a sharp reduction in the number of illegals heading north to find work. Over five years earlier, in an article in the *Wall Street Journal* headlined—are you ready for this?—"A

New Future for Mexico's Work Force: Hot Job Market Eases Pressure to go the U.S.," reporter Joel Millman found some undue optimism:

"For fifteen years, the number of working-age Mexicans entering the labor force has stayed the same, and we needed emigration to help our people find work," says demographer Augustin Escobar. "But now that we see growth of that working-age cohort is slowing, we can also see that the future is going to be quite different from what we saw in the 1980s and the 1990s."

The future he sees is one where the supply of new jobs in Mexico matches, or even exceeds, the number of annual entrants into the labor force. When that happens, he figures, Mexicans won't be as inclined to emigrate. Mr. Escobar, who works at Guadalajara's CIESAS think tank, calculates that day may come as soon as the year 2006. "My most pessimistic scenario," he says, "is the year 2010."[20]

Of course, here we are in 2006 and nothing of the kind has happened. Far from slowing, illegal immigration to the United States has skyrocketed since 2000, even as the Mexican economy has grown steadily with lower unemployment. In fact, 2005 likely will turn out to be the biggest year *ever* for illegal immigration. The only way Escobar's prediction will materialize is if Mexico pretty much clears out.

Here is a quick summation. In 2000, Escobar said demographics and a growing economy would quell the illegal invasion in five to ten years. In 2000, Mexican president Vicente Fox made the same argument, except he said it would take ten to fifteen years. Now Dowd comes along five years later and tells us that it will take twenty. Do I hear twenty-five?

Mark Krikorian further demolishes Dowd's fertility theory on National Review Online:

Russia has one of the lowest fertility rates in the world and yet continues to send large numbers of immigrants to the United States. Congo, on the other hand, has one of the highest fertility rates in the world, and sends few immigrants anywhere. Japan and South Korea both have extremely low fertility, and yet one sends lots of immigrants while the other doesn't. Or how about Brazil, whose fertility rate has fallen to about the U.S. level, but is only now becoming a major immigrant-sending country.[21]

What does Dowd say will happen after twenty years? Businesses that have relied on cheap illegal labor will "need to adapt by increasing salaries and benefits so they can attract legal immigrants or citizens as workers." Hire citizens? What a concept!

But why should low-income American workers have to wait another twenty years to get the higher wages and better benefits they should have *right now*? And why does business need a twenty-year labor subsidy paid by citizens through higher taxes, less diversity, more crime, a crippled health care system, failing schools, less security, and a general disrespect for the rule of law?

Dowd ends with this: "We should be aware of the historic transformations occurring in Mexican society so that we aren't fighting a war that is already ending." If we follow Dowd's advice, it is a "war" we are sure to lose.

CHAPTER EIGHT

IS ILLEGAL IMMIGRATION THE ANSWER TO SOCIAL SECURITY?

"Illegals are union-busters. They depress the minimum wage. They keep production costs low. And they bolster Social Security with uncollected millions of dollars taken out of every paycheck. A Mexican consul told me, 'We Mexicans are here to keep your retired people afloat.'"[1]

—Luis Alberto Urrea

BECAUSE SUPPORTERS of open borders and amnesty for illegal immigrants know the American people oppose them, they devise clever arguments that tie illegal immigration to some other social good. One such argument is that immigration, including the illegal variety, is the answer to the looming bankruptcy of Social Security.

Thus the *Wall Street Journal*'s editorial page proclaims, "The old and the new: immigrants play a key role in Social Security."[2] The *New York Times* chimes in, "Illegal immigrants are bolstering Social Security with billions."[3]

Even Mexican officials are getting in on the act. In a column in the *Arizona Republic*, author Luis Alberto Urrea wrote that illegals "bolster Social Security with uncollected millions of dollars taken out of every paycheck. A Mexican consul told me, 'We Mexicans are here to keep your retired people afloat.'"[4]

Actually, illegal immigration provides an illusory benefit to Social Security, and, if some in Washington have their way, could even become a huge drain on the system. As I am a member of the Social Security subcommittee in the House of Representatives, that possibility worries me.

Social Security, as we all know, is in serious trouble, and the longer we wait to address the problem, the more costly it will be. And it is true that *legal* immigration, if we go about it the right way, could help Social Security stay solvent. A study by the National Foundation for American Policy found that increasing legal immigration by 33 percent annually would reduce Social Security's actuarial deficit—its projected shortfall—by 10 percent, while a 20 percent increase per year would reduce it by 6 percent.[5]

Most immigrants come to America at a relatively young age. So they usually pay into the system for decades before they begin collecting benefits. But it matters greatly whether the immigrants are skilled (in which case they will likely contribute more in taxes than they receive in benefits) or unskilled (in which case their benefits normally exceed their contributions to the program).

Legal immigration of engineers, doctors, and high-tech entrepreneurs can be a legitimate strategy to strengthen Social Security. What about illegal immigration? That is a very different story. To understand why, we need to take a look at how the Social Security Administration (SSA) and the Internal Revenue Service (IRS) actually protect illegal workers and their employers. In doing so, they set the stage for an unprecedented and potentially devastating raid on the Social Security system.

THE FRAUD GAME

Illegal aliens have learned that the easiest way to get a job is to acquire "micas," or phony documents. Today in Phoenix an illegal can buy both a fake Social Security card and fake permanent residency card for less than $100. How good are they? After busting a document-counterfeiting ring in Phoenix, federal authorities said the bogus documents were so expertly done that "only a crime lab could distinguish them from the real thing."[6]

As a result, every year the SSA receives millions of earnings reports (better known as W-2s) with Social Security numbers that don't match its database. Many are the result of typographical errors or name changes due to marriage, but the vast majority likely belong to illegal aliens.

Of the top 100 companies submitting bad W-2s from 1997 to 2001, more than half were from three states with large illegal populations: California, Texas, and Illinois.[7] Coincidence? Hardly. Neither is it a coincidence that the sorts of businesses submitting most of the bad Social Security numbers are ones that hire lots of illegal aliens. According to the Government Accountability Office, just five of the industry categories (out of eighty-three) were responsible for 43 percent of earnings reports with bad Social Security numbers. And these industries were? It's not hard to guess: eating and drinking establishments, construction and special trades, agricultural production/crops, business service organizations, and health service organizations.[8]

One company, headquartered in Illinois, was responsible for 131,991 false earnings reports, the highest in the nation. A Texas company was second, with 108,302 bad reports, followed by one in Florida, with 106,073. Even more incredible is that a *state agency* made the list!

It is hard to believe that the companies and agencies filing so many bad reports don't know they are hiring illegal aliens. Ignorance is certainly no excuse. Here's why.

If the name and number on a W-2 don't correspond with its records, the SSA will send the employee (and in most cases, the employer) a "no-match" letter stating that there is a discrepancy and asking for corrected information. However, the actual language of the letter bends over backwards to give the benefit of the doubt to employers and their illegal workers. Here are some excerpts from a typical "no-match" letter:

> IMPORTANT: This letter does not imply that you or your employee intentionally gave the government wrong information about the employee's name or Social Security number. Nor does it make any statement about an employee's immigration status. We need corrected information.

You should not use this letter to take any adverse action against an employee just because his or her Social Security number appears on the list, such as laying off, suspending, firing, or discriminating against that individual. Doing so could, in fact, violate state and federal law and subject you to legal consequences.

It would be a great help to us if you could respond within sixty days with the information that you are able to correct.

But that is as far as it goes—employers are under no obligation to actually correct the error! How, or even if, they respond is entirely up to them. Some businesses will do the right thing, others won't. The *Arizona Republic* reports on an illegal alien named "Javier," the foreman of a framing crew: "Supervisors at two previous jobs discovered Javier was in the country illegally after receiving government notices that his Social Security number was bad. He was forced to quit both jobs. 'I don't know whether my employer suspects I'm illegal or not,' Javier said."[9]

Even more outrageous, despite the high probability that the vast majority of those with bad Social Security numbers are illegal aliens, is that the SSA is not allowed to share "no-match" information with the Department of Homeland Security, the agency charged with enforcing our immigration laws! That needs to change.

In 1993 President Bill Clinton nominated Zoe Baird for attorney general. She withdrew from consideration after it was disclosed that she had failed to pay Social Security taxes for her illegal nanny and chauffeur. In 2001 Linda Chavez withdrew as President George W. Bush's nominee for secretary of the Department of Labor after revelations that she housed an illegal alien. Then in 2004 President Bush nominated Bernard Kerik for secretary of Homeland Security. Kerik likewise withdrew after admitting that he did not pay Social Security taxes on an illegal nanny.

Between the three of them I count four illegal aliens. Yet that was enough to sink the public careers of three talented people. Meanwhile, companies that hire hundreds of thousands of illegal aliens don't even get a slap on the wrist. Something is not right.

Adding to the problem are left-wing groups like the pro–illegal immigrant National Immigration Law Center (NILC), which make sure employers don't get the wrong idea about these "no-match" letters. The NILC has put together a "Do-It-Yourself Packet for Immigrant Workers' Advocates" instructing them how to intimidate—or what it euphemistically calls "educate" and "effectively deal" with—employers on this issue. The program essentially consists of pointedly reminding employers of all the laws they could violate if they take action against any employee who is the subject of a "no-match" letter. The message is simple: employers might risk more by taking action against an employee flagged by the SSA than by ignoring the agency. The tactic works.

Raul Garcia-Gomez—the illegal alien who allegedly murdered a Denver detective (see Chapter Two)—was employed at a restaurant co-owned by Denver's Democratic mayor John Hickenlooper and was the subject of a "no-match" letter from the SSA. Responding to outraged citizens, the owners changed their hiring policy to require that new employees provide verifiable Social Security numbers.

The company's spokesman told the *Denver Post* that some applicants "changed their minds when told they must provide a verifiable Social Security number."[10] (You mean the mere prospect of enforcement works? Imagine that!) But the new policy does not cover workers already employed at the restaurants because the company claims it could be exposed to legal liability if it fires them. Immigration lawyer Ann Allott outlines the catch-22 nature of the dilemma: "They're caught between employment law and immigration law. The employment lawyer tells you can't go out and just can these people. The immigration lawyer says if they have a fake Social Security number, get rid of them."[11]

It is a pity that it took a brutal crime to get these people to do the right thing. But if Mayor Hickenlooper's restaurants can abide by the law with just a little extra effort, why can't every business in America?

MR. SOFTEE AND THE IRS

What about the bureaucrats over at the IRS? Surely they must have rules against filing phony tax documents?

They sure do. But the one agency that strikes fear into the hearts of most Americans and would pry a wooden nickel from the hand of your dead grandmother is a soft touch when it comes to fraud committed by illegal aliens and their employers.

Under federal law, the IRS can levy a fine of up to $50 for every W-2 containing incorrect information. However, employers, as usual, have been given a loophole. No penalty will be levied if an employer has exercised "due diligence" and can show "reasonable cause" for providing false information. In practice, that means asking the employee for corrected information—not actually getting corrected information, but just asking for it. And although employers may ask to see an employee's Social Security card, employees are not required to show the card if it is not available.

How big a loophole is this? The GAO found that the "IRS has no record of ever penalizing employers for filing inaccurate information on earnings statements."[12]

That's right. *Ever!* Millions of bad W-2s are filed every year and yet the big bad IRS has never collected a dime in fines.

It doesn't have to be this way. There is a program in place that allows employers to check on the validity of a potential hire's Social Security number almost instantaneously and at no cost. The U.S. Citizenship and Immigration Services (CIS) runs the Basic Pilot Employment Verification Program. Employers can log on to a government website and check a worker's documents (Social Security and alien registration numbers) against a government database. Usually, an employer can have an answer in just a few minutes.

Yet according to congressional testimony by James Lockhart, the deputy commissioner of the SSA, just 13,000 individual employer sites were using Basic Pilot as of January 1, 2004,[13] out of well over five million companies doing business in the United States. A CIS spokesman told the *Arizona Republic* that in my home state of Arizona, just 101 out of 96,000 employers in the state were using the program.[14] Why?

Two reasons. First, not many employers know about the program; it has only recently expanded to all fifty states. Second, and most important, the program is not mandatory. Since companies that use

Basic Pilot can be put at a competitive disadvantage with those that don't, it is not surprising that so many choose the bliss that comes with not knowing.

As it turns out, the IRS is also rather selective when choosing which of its rules to enforce. IRS rules for W-2s are the same as the rules for incorrect information on the 1099 forms that companies use to report earnings, such as interest and dividends, from which taxes have not been withheld. According to a GAO report, it enforces the law on Form 1099 vigorously.

Again, the reason is simple. Faulty 1099s bring in less tax revenue, so the IRS takes them seriously. However, getting tough on faulty W-2s might interfere with tax collections. The GAO found: "In discussing this issue, IRS officials expressed concern that requiring the verification of names and SSNs may cause some employers to cease withholding taxes and reporting income from unauthorized workers, rather than risk losing such workers."[15]

In other words, it all comes down to money.

The word "scandal" is overused, but for the federal government to look the other way while corporations openly hire millions of illegal aliens is truly a scandal. Far from trying to stop it, the SSA and the IRS have become enablers of illegal behavior. When confronted with their dereliction, they make pitiful excuses: "War on Terror? Sorry, not our job. We'll sit this one out." Haven't we learned anything since September 11? Enforcing our immigration laws has to be everyone's job.

HOW PAYING TAXES PAYS OFF FOR ILLEGALS

In fact, the tax scandal is even bigger. Illegal aliens have figured out how to game the IRS's Individual Taxpayer Identification Number (ITIN) system.

The IRS issues ITINs to individuals who owe taxes but are not eligible for a Social Security number, for example, foreign investors who are required to pay U.S. taxes. Since the inception of the program in July 1996, the IRS has issued well over eight million ITINs.

Illegals have discovered that they too can receive ITINs. At first, they only had to ask. Now they can apply for one only when filing a tax return. Why would illegal aliens want to file U.S. tax returns? Because, with a tax return, banks will offer them home loans and other financial services.

As usual, when confronted with evidence that illegal aliens are pulling a fast one by using these numbers for other purposes, IRS officials respond the only way they know how. In testimony before the Ways and Means Oversight subcommittee in March 2004, IRS commissioner Mark Everson came clean:

> We [the IRS] are fully sensitive to the possible dangers that can arise from the misuse of ITINs for the purpose of creating an identity, *including the possible threat to national security* [emphasis added]. Regardless of undesirable behaviors actually or potentially associated with ITINs, the Service remains legally responsible for enforcement of the nation's federal tax laws with respect to ITIN holders, including the responsibility to assess and impose tax on ITIN holders irrespective of the circumstances of their employment or the possibility that ITIN applicants may be solely or collaterally seeking the procurement of an ITIN to establish an identity for non-tax purposes.[16]

In other words, "Don't bother us about illegal aliens—including terrorists—using our number to make themselves legitmate. It's not our job. We're just here to collect taxes."

Look for the number of ITINs to explode in coming years as the word spreads about the IRS's latest benefit for illegal aliens.

IMPACT OF ILLEGAL IMMIGRATION: SOCIAL INSECURITY

Despite all this, we still hear that illegal immigrants are the answer to our Social Security woes, a proposition that has advocates on both sides of the aisle. On the surface, they have a point.

Steve Camarota of the Center for Immigration Studies has estimated that in 2002, households headed by illegal aliens generated some $6.4 billion in Social Security payroll taxes.[17] That means that every year, the IRS collects billions in Social Security taxes from illegal aliens; very few of whom, *under current law*, will ever collect Social Security benefits. But is this really a good thing?

While $6.4 billion might sound like a lot of money, it pales in comparison to the tremendous burden, financial and otherwise, illegal immigration puts on American taxpayers (see Chapter One). One of those burdens is the growing incidence of identity theft.

George Willis is an attorney and the program administrator of the Low Income Taxpayer Clinic at the Chapman University School of Law in Orange, California. He is also the victim of identity theft. He outlined a typical scenario in testimony submitted to the Ways and Means Oversight subcommittee:

> A potential worker in State X is unable to obtain a valid SSN. An employer tells the worker that they must have a SSN in order to work. The employer proposes that the worker use a SSN or ITIN that the employer happens to "have available," or in the alternative directs the taxpayer to some place where, for a price, they can "get one." The worker uses this SSN or ITIN and may or may not file a tax return.
>
> A year later, the valid SSN or ITIN holder in State Y is sent a bill by the Internal Revenue Service (IRS) for not reporting the wages earned in State X. The taxpayer in State Y comes to me, and we resolve the case over the course of one to two years.
>
> The employer claims ignorance to the whole thing and does not cooperate with the valid SSN holder, nor our clinic's requests, as there are no penalties for not cooperating.
>
> At the end of the case, the IRS and the SSA have not received monies owed to them. The valid SSN holder has negative marks on their credit report due to tax liens, et cetera. Our clinic expends hundreds of staff hours in this process. The invalid SSN holder continues to use the SSN and maybe even shares it with others, and the cycle continues year after year for the valid SSN holder.
>
> The illustration that I have provided certainly demonstrates that there is actual harm to the economy of the nation even in situations where there is no out-of-pocket-harm to the consumer.[18]

Take the real-life case of Barbara Vidlak of Omaha, Nebraska. According to a story in the *Omaha-World Herald*, a phony Social Security card with her name and number was sold to an illegal alien who also happened to be living and working in Omaha. That's when her troubles began. Vidlak, a divorced mother of two, discovered the fraud when she received a letter from the government stating that her young children could no longer receive public health insurance because she earned too much.

Vidlak conducted her own investigation and found that an illegal alien, Maria Delgadillo of Mexico, was using her name and Social Security number. Delgadillo was subsequently deported. She left her U.S.-born baby behind to live with its father, also an illegal alien. In many ways Delgadillo's story is tragic.

Meanwhile, Vidlak was forced to incur burdensome expenses for credit checks, to protect the validity of her Social Security status, and other expenses, such as lost time at work. Adding insult to injury, when a stressed Vidlak asked the SSA for a new Social Security number, she was denied. Vidlak is justifiably outraged by what happened and believes the system let her down.

Yet the pro–illegal alien lobby, as usual, tried to make *Delgadillo* the victim. Ed Leahy of the Immigrant Rights Network in Nebraska told the *Omaha-World Herald*, "We've got people having to live lies to be able to do the very basic things. I wish this country would step up to the plate and say, 'We need the people to do these jobs'—because we do."[19]

The story continued, "In some ways, Leahy said, both women are victims."

You could see that one coming a mile off, couldn't you? But the unpleasant fact is that only one of these two "victims" *broke the law*!

When you cut through all the politically correct nonsense, this was a simple case of identity theft, and I cannot imagine that anyone would be calling Delgadillo a victim and making excuses for her if she were not an illegal alien. To quote Barbara Vidlak, "This is bull." Bull, indeed.

Identity theft is a serious and growing problem in this country, so it is likely we will hear more of these kinds of stories in the future... and the same lame excuses for lawlessness from the likes of Ed Leahy.

TOTALLY CRAZY

Perhaps the biggest threat to Social Security comes from the "totalization" agreement that the Bush administration has negotiated with Mexico (not yet approved).

"Totalization" is one of those words only a policy wonk could have dreamed up. It is the term used for agreements that coordinate our Social Security system with comparable programs in other countries. Under such agreements, American workers and their companies pay Social Security taxes in just one country instead of both. The same applies for foreigners working here. Under totalization, Social Security will pay foreigners prorated benefits based on the number of years they paid into our system (just eighteen months are required to qualify for benefits).

The United States currently has twenty totalization agreements with other countries, all advanced industrial economies with stable democratic governments. For the most part, these agreements pose very few problems to Social Security because of the small number of workers involved. The same can't be said of our agreement with Mexico.

According to the SSA, over the first five years of totalization, Mexico would send $29 million to American workers while we would send $550 million to Mexican workers. Mexico actively encourages its citizens to illegally invade our country; it regularly opposes the U.S. at the United Nations, including opposing our effort in Iraq; and it refuses to extradite to the U.S. some of the most notorious criminals to be tried in American courts. Has Mexico been a good enough neighbor to merit a totalization agreement that provides far greater benefits to its citizens than it does to ours? Don't we subsidize the Mexicans enough?

Shortly after negotiations with Mexico concluded, I met with Social Security commissioner Jo Anne Barnhart to voice my deep concern. Barnhart is an able administrator and is very knowledgeable, yet after our discussion I was more convinced than ever that there are serious problems with this agreement.

Leading the list of concerns is the absurd assumption on the part of the SSA that only 50,000 of the millions of Mexican workers, legal and illegal, in the U.S. will initially qualify for Social Security benefits under this agreement. Equally absurd is the prediction that even with millions of Mexican workers totalization with Mexico will cost less than our agreement with Canada!

A Government Accountability Office report confirmed my doubts, concluding that "the cost of a totalization agreement with Mexico is highly uncertain" because of the large number of illegal Mexican workers in the U.S. It notes that if the actual number of eligible Mexican beneficiaries were just 25 percent above that 50,000 estimate, or 63,000, it would have "a measurable impact on the long-range actuarial balance of the trust funds."[20]

So if the actuaries underestimate by just 13,000 beneficiaries, Social Security would be seriously and negatively impacted. Do we really want to put Social Security at greater risk by finalizing an agreement whose initial cost is "highly uncertain"? Uncertainty is the last thing we need when we're dealing with the future of Social Security!

THE SAND, THE SURF, THE SOCIAL SECURITY CHECK

Believe it or not, prior to 2004, if illegal aliens could prove that they worked the requisite number of quarters, even on a phony Social Security number, they were entitled to benefits—without even having to become legal. The Social Security Protection Act of 2004 changed that. Now the only way illegal aliens can collect Social Security benefits is by becoming legal, through amnesty or marriage to an American citizen, for example. Once legalized, they would be able to receive benefits based on both their legal and *illegal* years of work!

Now contemplate what would happen if we finalized a totalization agreement with Mexico and then enacted a guest-worker program legalizing millions of currently illegal workers and their family members. Not only would legalized guest workers get credit for work they did while illegal, but family members would be eligible for benefits without ever having set foot in the United States, legally or otherwise.

Totalization would also bring up a whole different set of problems. Here's the GAO again: "SSA provided no information showing that it assessed the reliability of Mexican earnings data and the internal controls in place to ensure the integrity of information that SSA will rely on to pay Social Security benefits."[21]

In other words, to determine whether Mexicans are eligible for benefits, the SSA will have to rely on Mexican earnings data as well as birth, death, and marriage records. This is an invitation to fraud on a colossal scale. We have been down this road before. A Congressional Research Service report states:

> [In 1979 the] Social Security commissioner stated that SSA investigators had found evidence that some recipients living abroad were faking marriages and adoptions and failing to report deaths in order to "cheat the system." At the time, the commissioner stated that such problems were particularly acute in Greece, Italy, Mexico, and the Philippines, where large numbers of beneficiaries were residing. He stated further that, in some countries, "there is a kind of industry built up of so-called claims-fixers who, for a percentage of the benefit, will work to ensure that somebody gets the maximum benefit they can possibly get out of the system."[22]

SSA commissioner Barnhart told me that her people have thoroughly examined Mexico's social security operations data collection and storage systems and have visited Mexican social security field offices. Barnhart said she is satisfied that Mexico is prepared to administer the agreement. In some ways, she said, their system is more up-to-date than ours.

But when a Mexican beneficiary dies in some small town in a rural part of Mexico, how is anyone at SSA going to know? Since the Mexican economy survives on remittances from the United States, who in Mexico would have an incentive to bring it to SSA's attention? The family members living off the checks? The Mexican government?

Then there are scams that not even good record-keeping can stop. For instance, many legal immigrants rent their Social Security numbers to illegals. The *New York Times* detailed how this benefits both parties:

> Hundreds of thousands of immigrants who cross the border from Mexico illegally each year need to procure a legal identity that will allow them to work in the United States. Many legal immigrants, whether living in the United States or back in Mexico, are happy to provide them: as they pad their earnings by letting illegal immigrants work under their name and number, they also enhance their own unemployment and pension benefits. And sometimes they charge for the favor.[23]

Imagine if you could qualify for Social Security benefits or increase your benefits on the back of someone else's labor. Sounds like a pretty sweet deal, doesn't it? Regrettably, as the *Times* noted, so long as tax returns and other documents are properly filed, neither the SSA nor the IRS is likely to detect the fraud.

JUST SAY NO TO TOTALIZATION

Besides posing a serious threat to the future solvency of Social Security, totalization would also act as an additional incentive for Mexicans to enter the United States illegally. Yet the SSA contends that few Mexican citizens would be motivated to come here by the prospect of future Social Security benefits because they are far more interested in current earnings.

This ignores the long history of illegal aliens "gaming the system" and turning our laws to their advantage, with most scams driven by word of mouth or information campaigns mounted by the Mexican government. At the very least, word will get out that illegal aliens should start saving their pay stubs or W-2 forms just in case. Many already do.

The *Wall Street Journal* reports on an illegal Mexican couple in Wisconsin, the Garcias, who were approved for a home mortgage with the help of an ITIN. When Mr. Garcia visited the bank to discuss the loan, he brought with him "pay stubs to show he earns $450 a week making concrete molding to secure caskets in the earth, a job he has held for four years."[24] The article goes on to say that Mrs. Garcia "carefully stores bills in a safe place, amassed the receipts for every utility and rent payment the couple had ever made."[25] They even brought proof that they had filed tax returns.

If Mr. Garcia were legalized under a guest-worker plan, he would be credited for his illegal work and would already qualify for Social Security benefits under totalization. His wife would qualify for survivor benefits. How many other millions of illegals would similarly qualify is impossible to say, but shouldn't we err on the side of caution when dealing with Social Security's future?

Although the totalization agreement was signed in June 2004, the SSA says it is still under review to ensure that it is fully consistent with American law. Eventually, the president will have to submit it to Congress, which has sixty days to kill it through a resolution of disapproval passed by either the House or Senate. That's how the law is written, but the law might not matter, because the Supreme Court has ruled that allowing just one chamber of Congress to exercise such authority is an unconstitutional legislative veto. So if the House or Senate or both voted to disapprove the agreement, a legal challenge would almost certainly follow.

Where does that leave us? What can we do to prevent this huge giveaway to illegal aliens?

We have only three realistic choices.

1. We can try to convince the president to abandon the agreement that his own administration negotiated.
2. We can amend the process and require the approval of both houses and the president for any totalization agreement.
3. We can pass legislation to deny the Social Security Administration the funds necessary to implement the agreement.

I have been working on all these fronts. I've written to the president asking him not to go forward with the agreement; I've introduced legislation to change the process; I've offered amendments to deny funding to the SSA to implement the agreement; I've vigorously denounced the legalization of illegal aliens via a guest-worker scheme. The bottom line is that *no one should receive a government benefit by breaking the law.*

That sounds like common sense. But the only way for common sense to win in Washington is for the American people to get involved and demand action from Congress. Otherwise, Washington will give away your future.

CHAPTER NINE

GUEST WORKER = AMNESTY = SURRENDER

"We asked for workers, and we got people."

—Author and playwright Max
Frisch on Germany's failed
guest-worker program

O N JANUARY 7, 2004, President George W. Bush gave an address on immigration policy in the East Room at the White House. In his speech, the president called for "an immigration system that serves the American economy, and reflects the American Dream." He went on to sum up his thinking on this issue with a formulation that has become a mantra: "I propose a new temporary worker program that will match willing foreign workers with willing American employers, when no Americans can be found to fill the jobs."

The president said his plan was based on four principles:

1. America must control its borders.
2. New immigration laws should serve the American economy.
3. We should not give unfair rewards to illegal immigrants in the citizenship process or disadvantage those who came here lawfully.
4. New laws should provide incentives for temporary, foreign workers to return permanently to their home countries after their period of work in the United States has expired.

He went on to propose a guest-worker program that would give illegal aliens the opportunity to live and work legally in the United States and eventually become citizens. Since the president's speech, several immigration reform bills have been introduced in Congress. The bill most closely resembling the president's initial outline was introduced in the House by Republicans Jim Kolbe and Jeff Flake of Arizona and Democrat Luis Gutierrez of Illinois, and in the Senate by Republican John McCain of Arizona and Democrat Ted Kennedy of Massachusetts.

Most commonly referred to as McCain-Kennedy, the bill would let the millions of illegal aliens already in the country with an offer of employment apply for a new visa, called an H-5B, which would allow them to work in the United States as a "non-immigrant." Visa holders could work for up to six years and would be allowed to travel abroad. To qualify for the program, illegals would have to submit to fingerprinting and a background check and pay a $1,000 fine, processing fees, and back taxes. Crimes related to immigration status or document fraud would not be held against them. Guest workers could also apply for citizenship but would not be given preferential treatment. To get a green card, workers would have to pay another $1,000 fine, undergo more criminal checks and a medical exam, register for Selective Service, and become proficient in English.

Ironically, McCain-Kennedy would provide for a minimum of 400,000 additional guest workers every year (on top of the millions already here), which is roughly the same number of illegal alien absconders with deportation orders. While several of the sponsors of McCain-Kennedy strenuously oppose the CLEAR Act, which would allow local law enforcement to help track down these 400,000 fugitives, they think nothing of building a whole new bureaucracy to track the movements of 400,000 new guest workers *every year*. A strange set of priorities.

Several other guest-worker proposals have been introduced that are based on the same assumptions and promise the same benefits. Guest-worker proponents tell us the concept will stop human smuggling and the flood of illegals crossing our border, put an end to the border deaths, increase government revenue by getting illegals to pay taxes, and lead to better wages and working conditions for guest workers *and* for Americans. They say it will enhance national security by letting us know who is in the country and where they are. And since guest workers will no longer fear deportation, they will be more likely to cooperate with police, which will help fight crime. Guest workers will be also more likely to have health insurance, benefiting our health care system. And, of course, they claim it will provide the workers America needs to do the jobs Americans won't.

In the interests of full disclosure I must tell you that at one time I supported a guest-worker scheme. However, after a thorough review of America's experience with similar programs, I have concluded that a guest-worker program would do nothing to solve our illegal immigration problem and would, in fact, make the problem worse by rewarding illegal behavior and encouraging even more illegal immigration.

"Matching willing workers with willing employers" is not a policy, it is a buzz phrase that really means, "We can't stop illegal immigration so we might as well legalize it." It is a way for the government to sweep its dereliction under the rug.

A guest-worker plan is wrong for our country. Here's why.

HAVE GUEST-WORKER PROGRAMS WORKED IN THE PAST?

One provision of McCain-Kennedy calls for a commission to evaluate the impact of the plan on the U.S. labor market. But we already have loads of empirical evidence on precisely these types of temporary-worker programs. As Dr. Vernon Briggs, a professor of industrial and labor relations at Cornell University, put it in testimony before the Senate Judiciary Committee: "Because [temporary-worker programs] have been undertaken in the past, they have a track record. They have been the subject of extensive research. There is no need to speculate about what might happen if any new such venture—such as that proposed by the Bush administration on January 7, 2004—were to be enacted. The outcome can be predicted."[1]

And based on past experience, the predictions are all *bad*. Yet the lessons of history seem lost on the latest crop of guest-worker advocates. For them, there is no education in the second, third, or even fourth kick of a mule.

In the earliest example of this type of scheme, guest workers were used as part of a national emergency program during World War I to pick crops. Known as the bracero program, it allowed farmers in the Southwest to recruit and hire unskilled Mexican workers. It was later expanded to allow work in non-farm environments, such as factories. Although they were supposed to return home once their work was finished, some 45 percent of the Mexican workers never left.

The second bracero program, formally known as the Mexican Labor Program, was established in 1942 to help the U.S. cope with labor shortage during World War II. The program officially ended at the end of 1947, but continued unofficially for many years afterward, prompting a presidential commission to examine the issue of migratory workers. Dr. Briggs noted in his testimony, "In its thorough report on the bracero program in 1952, President Truman's Commission on Migratory Labor found that 'wages by states [to agricultural workers] were inversely related to the supply of alien labor.'"[2]

In other words, the higher the number of bracero workers, the lower the wages paid to American workers. The Truman Commission report would be the first of many to conclude that temporary-worker programs were bad for American workers and bad for the American economy.

Still, the bracero program idea was resurrected in 1951 because of a labor shortage during the Korean War. But by the early 1960s, President John F. Kennedy determined the program was "adversely affecting the wages, working conditions, and employment opportunities of our own agricultural workers" and began phasing it out.[3] It was permanently ended at the end of 1964 by President Lyndon Johnson.

In the late 1970s, President Jimmy Carter asked the National Commission for Manpower Policy to study whether the H-2 temporary-worker program should be expanded as a way to give employers an alternative to illegal aliens. In May 1979, the commission's chairman advised the president that he was "strongly against" any such expansion for the usual reasons:

1. Cheap foreign labor is addictive.
2. It would be another bracero program.
3. The government does not have the ability to manage a larger program.
4. It wouldn't slow illegal immigration.

Congress was also considering a guest-worker scheme around this time. In 1978, it established the Select Commission on Immigration and Refugee Policy to examine all aspects of our immigration policy and to make recommendations for change. Chairing the commission was the Reverend Theodore Hesburgh, the distinguished former president of Notre Dame University and a well-known political liberal who represents a church sympathetic to illegal immigrants.

Hesburgh called a guest-worker plan "seductive" and said that he was "entranced" by it, but after careful study was persuaded it would be a mistake.[4] He concluded: "We do not think it wise to propose a program with potentially harmful consequences to the United States as a whole."[5]

In 1990 Congress passed an immigration law establishing yet another bipartisan commission to look into the issue. This one was chaired by Barbara Jordan, another liberal and the first African American woman to serve in Congress. The Jordan Commission said it would be a "grievous mistake" to assume that a guest-worker program would alleviate the problem of illegal immigration, and argued that such a program would depress wages for low-skilled American workers, exploit foreign workers, increase taxpayer costs for health care and other services, and actually encourage more illegal immigration.

Despite the mountain of evidence saying they don't work, the calls for a guest-worker scheme kept coming, prompting this response from President Bill Clinton:

I oppose efforts in Congress to institute a new guest-worker or "bracero" program that seeks to bring thousands of foreign workers into the United States to provide temporary farm labor.... A new guest-worker program is unwarranted for several reasons:

1. It would increase illegal immigration.
2. It would reduce work opportunities for U.S. citizens and other legal residents.
3. It would depress wages and work standards for American workers.

When these programs were tried in the past, many temporary guest workers stayed permanently—and illegally—in this country. Hundreds of thousands of immigrants now residing in the U.S. first came as temporary workers, and their presence became a magnet for other illegal immigrants.[6]

If liberals like Theodore Hesburgh, Barbara Jordan, and Bill Clinton could understand these facts, why do so many conservatives remain so obtuse? And why have so many liberals abandoned their commitment to looking out for American workers?

It has often been said that the clinical definition of insanity is doing the same thing over and over again and expecting a different result. By that definition the proposals to give a guest-worker program just one more shot are, not to put too fine a point on it, *INSANE!*

And yet the politicians never give up on them.

FACTS ON THE GROUND

Advocates claim that extending legal status to those currently working illegally in this country simply recognizes the "facts on the ground." There are already eleven to twenty million illegals here, the argument goes, and rounding them up and sending them home is unrealistic. They say opponents like me "mischaracterize" their plan as an "amnesty." Maybe they would prefer "surrender."

But compare the guest-worker notion to a tax amnesty, which gives tax evaders one last chance to comply with the law before the IRS goes after them. In 2002, Arizona had just such a tax amnesty. Tax evaders were given a final opportunity to pay up before facing almost certain detection using sophisticated new computers. It was a huge success, with the state collecting about three times what was predicted.

The guest-worker crowd would turn that approach on its head. Instead of giving illegals a chance to conform to the law, they would change the law to conform to the aliens' illegal behavior. Guest-worker proponents have admitted as much. Writing in the *Weekly Standard*, the Manhattan Institute's Tamar Jacoby was blunt: "Far simpler to bring the law back into line with market reality, then implement the new rules with modest, commonsense enforcement measures of the sort we rely on in every other realm of American life."[7]

Ken Mehlman, the chairman of the Republican National Committee, made a similar argument in an e-mail to a conservative supporter: "Conservatives have always understood that laws don't work when they ignore market realities. In this case, the market reality is that there are jobs Americans don't want but we need done."

But are we dealing with market reality... or marked absurdity?

Again, illegals aren't taking jobs Americans won't; they're taking *wages* Americans won't. The *Wall Street Journal* may call this a "flexible labor market,"[8] but the rest of us know it really amounts to "open borders." After all, once you allow unfettered competition between American workers and illegal aliens, where does it end?

Furthermore, why should "market realities" drive labor markets but not the market for goods? For example, should we do away with anti-dumping laws that protect American producers from being undercut by foreign companies selling goods at below the cost of production? I'm a pretty staunch free-trader, but I'd never support repealing our anti-dumping laws. And illegal immigration is akin to poor countries "dumping" their cheap, excess labor into our economy, to the detriment of our workers.

Illegal immigration is not a market reality—it is a market *distortion*. You simply cannot allow unfettered competition for labor between an advanced economy like ours and the struggling, inefficient, and often backward economies you find in places like Central America and Mexico.

Under any kind of guest-worker plan, an employer would be crazy to offer a job at anything above the minimum wage, knowing that if no American wants it at that price there will be plenty of desperate foreigners clamoring to take it. As Ruben Navarette so aptly puts it, "Guest workers are nothing but a glorified labor subsidy to farms, restaurants, construction firms, and other industries hooked on illegal immigration labor—one that often leaves workers abused and exploited."[9]

Talk about corporate welfare! The result will be a permanent and growing underclass of minimum-wage workers. For lower-income Americans, the competition with cheap imported labor makes the American Dream almost unattainable. And that is a tragedy.

FEE OR FINE?

Some call it "amnesty-lite." Others call it "amnesty on the installment plan." But there is no doubt that the guest-worker plan proposed by the president and reflected in McCain-Kennedy is amnesty. Period.

Proponents have the audacity to claim the plan is not amnesty because it doesn't, in the president's words, "place undocumented workers on the automatic path to citizenship." But what does citizenship have to do with it?

Illegals don't come here because they want to be American citizens. They don't come here having memorized the Constitution, studied American history, or become proficient in English. They come here because they want to work. If we allow them to do what they came here to do in the first place—i.e., work—that's *amnesty*.

Guest-worker proponents say it's not amnesty because, in the words of the *Arizona Republic* editorial board, "in order to achieve guest-worker status, these immigrants have to pay a stiff fine."[10] The "stiff fine"? A paltry $1,000 ($2,000 if you go for citizenship too). Workers would even be allowed to pay in installments.

Tellingly, the president initially couldn't bring himself to call this a "fine," which would at least acknowledge some degree of wrongdoing. Instead, he called it a "fee." But it's neither fee nor fine—it's a *bargain*.

By itself, using a fake Social Security number is a felony punishable by a fine of up to $250,000 and/or up to five years' imprisonment. The various guest-worker proposals pardon illegals for that offense as well as all other document-related fraud. Cha-ching.

But wait, there's more. (I'm starting to sound like one of those hucksters on late-night television.) Once legalized, guest workers will be able to have what they've earned using a phony Social Security number count toward Social Security benefits for themselves and their survivors. Break the law—or several—and get a check!

We are harangued ad nauseum that illegal aliens, in the words of Ted Kennedy, "risk great danger, and even death, to cross our borders."[11] But a $1,000 fine is far less than what illegals are paying smugglers for the privilege of taking such risks. The *Arizona Republic* reported that "smugglers typically charge $1,500 or more to guide migrants across the border." Jorge Castillo, a Guatemalan who has made the journey across the Arizona desert seven times in seven years, told the *New York Times*, "It should not cost more than $2,000...to go from the Mexican side of the border to Phoenix." A Guatemalan illegal told the *Washington Post* he paid a coyote "$2,400 to get him to California." Depending on how far south an immigrant starts, the going rate can jump to $5,000 or more.

The idea that this $1,000 "fee" is onerous is a joke. As *National Review* rightly put it, "The putative fine is little more than a retroactive smuggling fee paid to the U.S. government."[12] Let's call it Uncle Sam's piece of the action.

If you still don't believe that a puny $1,000 fine amounts to a reward for illegals, what do you think would happen if we set up a booth at the border offering entry to the United States at that price? My guess is the line would stretch from Nogales to Buenos Aires.

What about the additional $1,000 "fee" for a path to citizenship? Compared to what legal immigrants pay, it's downright cheap. According to a Phoenix immigration attorney who handles family-based immigration petitions, which make up the majority of immigration cases, a very conservative estimate for an immigration attorney to see a case through to permanent residency is $2,500. The cost of an employment-based application, which is usually picked up by the company, is even more.

Most likely, legal immigrants will pay much, much more. Participating in a town-hall meeting on how Hispanic parents can improve their children's education, columnist Ruben Navarette caused a stir when he said that if illegal aliens wanted the same educational benefits available to American citizens, they should try to become legal:

> I told the crowd that I knew of one person who spent twelve years and more than $12,000 to convert her status, and that of her son, from "illegal" to "legal." That brought gasps. Apparently, that sounded like a lot of money. It isn't, I told them. It's $1,000 per year, or about $80 a month. I know immigrants who spend that on their monthly cell phone bill, and this is much more important.[13]

A fine of $1,000 to work in the United States for six years comes to less than $14 a month; $2,000 for work and permanent residence to less than $28. This is "stiff"?

The fact is that a truly punitive fine would defeat one of the goals of the guest-worker plan—bringing illegal aliens out of the shadows. Kevin Rogers, president of the Arizona Farm Bureau, writes in the *Arizona Republic*, "Farm Bureau opposes amnesty, but we do support a pathway which will encourage perhaps ten million to fourteen million people to emerge from the shadows, allow for identification, and to provide for mechanisms for proper temporary status, which could lead to legal status. These mechanisms should not suggest reward, but if too punitive will drive people further underground."[14]

Guest-worker advocates should just be honest about what it is they want: a blanket amnesty with a minimum of bother for illegal aliens and the businesses that hire them.

THE SUPER BOWL OF ABSURDITY

The absurd fine—excuse me, "fee"—that guest-worker advocates tout would turn illegals that by law should be sent home into legal workers that can remain here for years, probably indefinitely. That's like saying if some folks get caught sneaking into the Super Bowl, just hit them with a small fine... but let them stay to watch the game. If that's not amnesty, I don't know what is.

Yet you will not get a single guest-worker supporter ever to admit that their plan is de facto amnesty. It's understandable. They see the polls showing that Americans oppose amnesty by huge margins. In fact, after testing the term on focus groups, the pro-amnesty National Council of La Raza "recommended to Mexican president Vicente Fox that he not utter the 'A' word."[15] It's advice Fox has followed assiduously.

As a result, amnesty proponents will do back flips to convince us that they aren't pushing amnesty. So they try to fool us with descriptions like "regularization," "legalization," and "earned status adjustments." In one of the 2004 presidential debates, John Kerry called for "earned legalization."

For his part, John McCain tackles the problem head-on with his trademark straight talk when he told the *Tucson Citizen*: "We think we have a workable proposal, Kennedy and I, that has bipartisan support— a lot of it—that says [illegals] have to pay a $2,000 fine, they have to work for six years before they can even be eligible for a green card, then they have to wait another five years before they can be citizens. If that's amnesty, I'm a Martian."[16]

Ted Kennedy, meanwhile, tries a little verbal sleight-of-hand: "Despite our compromises and bipartisan solutions, there are many who oppose these reforms. They misleadingly categorize our efforts as 'immigrant amnesty.' They refuse to accept that these reforms simply create a legalization for U.S. workers who have already been residing and working in the U.S."[17]

This is a version of "You say potato, I say potahto (given Kennedy's accent, I suppose it should be the other way around), let's call the whole thing off!"

Earth to Ted: trust me when I say that we *do* accept that your reforms create a legalization scheme—*that's why we call it an amnesty!*

This is a repeat of the debate on the 1986 immigration bill, when the words "legalization" and "amnesty" were used interchangeably, such as when sponsor Alan Simpson said of his own bill, "Because it is called legalization, or amnesty, it seems to stick in the craw of Americans."[18] Senator Jeremiah Denton said, "The second area which gives me reason for concern is the legalization or amnesty provision."[19] On and on it goes.

Any fair-minded person understands that "legalization" is amnesty. But don't take my word for it. In 2001, La Raza president Raul Yzaguirre said of the distinction between amnesty and legalization: "The net effect is the same."[20] For once, we agree.

Y'ALL COME NOW, HEAR!

Let's take the Super Bowl analogy a little further. I am sure that every year there are a few crazies who try to sneak into the big game. Suppose a rumor began circulating that sneaking into the stadium was easy and that once inside, officials would let you stay to watch the game if you paid a small fine amounting to less than the price of a ticket. Do you think more or fewer people would try?

That is essentially what happened after the president announced his guest-worker plan. In Mexico, Central America, and elsewhere the proposal was seen as almost an open invitation to head north. Since that time our borders have been overrun.

Of course, the Bush administration denies that the president's proposal was the cause of the stampede, but that just flies in the face of the facts. One Arizona rancher along the border, George Morin, who deals with this problem every day, told *Time* magazine: "All these people say they are coming for the amnesty program. [They] have been told if they get ten miles off the border, they are home free."[21]

Luis Alberto Urrea, author of *The Devil's Highway*, the tragic story of a group of illegal aliens trying to cross into Arizona, wrote: "[W]alkers come north faster for many reasons. They believe President Bush is going to grant them amnesty and, if they rush, they can beat the imaginary deadline that seems to constantly be looming a month or two away."[22]

Not long after Bush's speech, the *Wall Street Journal* reported:

Agents on the border argue that report of new work-visa regulations have morphed into wild rumors of amnesty, rumors that are triggering the northbound rush. "When the president made this announcement, every Border Patrol agent said this would happen," said Joseph Dassaro, president of Local 1613 of the Border Patrol agent's union. Added another border official, who didn't want to be identified by name, "Down there someone reads that George Bush and Vicente Fox made a deal and he thinks, 'Bush said I could have a job.'"[23]

But maybe the best evidence that the president's proposal caused a flood of illegal immigration is from the Bush administration itself. After the president's guest-worker speech, the Border Patrol was ordered to interview apprehended illegals to find out whether the president's policy encouraged them to cross the border. Legal watchdog group Judicial Watch acquired the survey after filing a Freedom of Information Act request. Among the findings:

- 45 percent crossed illegally based on rumors of a Bush administration amnesty
- 63 percent received Mexican government or media information supporting the notion of a Bush administration amnesty
- 80 percent desired to apply for amnesty
- 66 percent decided to petition for family members to join them in the United States[24]

I could have told the president as much without a survey. In fact, I did. Here's what I said during an appearance with Neil Cavuto on FOX News the day of the president's speech:

With all due respect to the president, he outlined and said this was no amnesty. He defined amnesty as taking folks, letting them jump in line and become citizens. I think you have to redefine amnesty. And it should be in this fashion: when you suddenly say to undocumented workers, to illegal workers, "You are legal," that is amnesty.

And it is wrong, because it does not enforce existing law. Essentially what the president has said today is two words: y'all come.

And come they did. President Bush may not have meant to start an illegal stampede, but there is no doubt he did. We can either do nothing and get trampled, or we can take corrective action now to get the situation under control.

FAMILY VALUES AND ILLEGAL ALIENS

At the Summit of the Americas in 2004, President Bush told reporters that most of the workers hired under his plan would have to return "permanently" to their home countries after their work period expired. The authors of the McCain-Kennedy immigration plan likewise insist that any guest workers will have to leave the country once their six-year work visa is up (unless they qualify for permanent residency). This is silly.

Illegal immigrants won't leave, they'll just shift back to the underground economy. Illegals are used to working outside the law, both in this country and in Mexico, where anywhere from 40 to 70 percent of the people work off the books. (Maybe Mexico needs a guest-worker plan for its own people.) Unless guest-worker proponents are willing to make life more difficult for those who refuse to leave—a dubious assumption, as we'll see—they won't go anywhere.

History has shown that there is a whole lot of truth to the old cliché "there is nothing more permanent than a temporary worker," a phenomenon that usually leads to serious long-term problems for the host country. In the midst of the riots outside Paris in fall 2005, France-based foreign correspondent Richard Z. Chesnoff wrote: "The problem originated in the 1950s and 1960s, when France began importing cheap labor from its former colonies in North Africa. *Les Arabes* were to do the dirty work and eventually go home. [Sound familiar?] Few did, and today North African immigrants and their families number almost six million, more than 10 percent of the French population."[25]

What makes anyone believe it would be different here? Remember, some 45 percent of Mexican workers brought in under the first bracero program never left.

More recently, when the Pew Hispanic Center asked Mexican "migrants" how long they expected to remain in the U.S., "a majority of respondents picked either 'as long as I can' (42 percent) or 'for the rest of my life' (17 percent)."[26] And after a speech in Tucson by President Bush promoting his "temporary" worker plan, an illegal alien told the *Arizona Republic*, "I don't believe it's realistic. The workers want to stay. They have lives here."[27]

Even workers who plan to return home eventually rarely do. The papers are full of stories of illegals who only intended to be in the United States for a few years—but never seem to leave. The *New York Times* ran a story comparing and contrasting the lives of an illegal Greek immigrant who came here in 1953 and an illegal Mexican immigrant who came here in 1990. It says of Mexican illegal aliens today: "Resentment and race subtly stand in their way, as does a lingering attachment to Mexico, which is so close that many immigrants do not put down deep roots here. They say they plan to stay only long enough to make some money and then go back home. Few ever do."[28]

One of the principal arguments for a guest-worker program is that illegal aliens are an important part of the American workforce and our economy needs them. Are we supposed to believe that we won't need these same workers in six years, at which time they would be required to leave? And when it becomes clear that guest workers aren't leaving as planned, will all those now promoting this discredited idea be out there leading the calls to round them up...or grant them amnesty?

The idea that illegal aliens will return home at the end of their work period is even more blinkered when you consider another provision the guest-worker crowd wants: family reunions.

Because the president sincerely believes that family values don't stop at the border (almost nothing does these days), he and others think we should allow the families of guest workers to come live in the United States as well. While this gesture illustrates President Bush's humanity, it is simply unworkable.

Any child born in the United States to guest-worker families would automatically be an American citizen. And once workers put down legal roots in this country, what incentive will they have to return home? Ever? Why should they?

Suppose you were a guest worker and during your stint you and your spouse had a child. Would you voluntarily leave the U.S.—with all its education and health benefits and almost unlimited opportunity—to return to Mexico? Or would you be more determined than ever to stay in the U.S. so that your child could have the opportunities you never did? The *Arizona Republic* tells us about one illegal couple, Cecelia and Jose, expecting their first child:

> Even with so much time invested living and working in the United States, they still dream of returning to Mexico some day, despite the hardships. "We miss the culture and the customs," Cecelia says. But with a baby on the way, Cecelia and Jose seem unlikely to return to Mexico. The United States will be their daughter's country, not Mexico. And as a U.S. citizen, the baby will have far more opportunities here than in Mexico, they said.[29]

They don't call them "anchor babies" for nothing.

If you want to know how heavy the anchor can be, consider the extreme case of Christian Higuera, who, as of this writing, is serving time in an Arizona jail for assault. Higuera fathered an illegitimate child born in Arizona, which makes the infant an American citizen. According to FOX News, Higuera "said he hopes he will be allowed to stay with his child...once he gets out of jail."[30]

Ponder that for a moment. An illegal alien and convicted felon actually harbors the hope that he will be allowed to stay in the United States once he gets out of jail simply because his illegitimate child is an American citizen! And who knows: if the past is any guide, he just might be able to pull it off.

But if a loser like Higuera doesn't think he'll have to head for home once he serves his sentence, what makes anyone believe some guest worker with an expired temporary work visa is just going to pack up and leave after experiencing what America has to offer for six years? It is preposterous.

BELGIAN PROSTITUTES AND SPANISH AMNESTY

Guest-worker proponents assure us that a properly administered program will curtail illegal immigration and allow the Border Patrol to concentrate on catching terrorists, drug smugglers, and other criminals.

But the government is simply not capable of managing a major guest-worker program that would require it to keep tabs on millions of people. A 2004 report issued by the U.S.-Mexico Binational Council says attempting a guest-worker program would be "a recipe for failure." It cited "serious shortcomings" in the way federal officials currently run the H-2A and H-2B temporary-worker programs, which are far smaller than any of the guest-worker plans now being contemplated.[31] And yet many farmers who complain the H-2A program is too bureaucratic and cumbersome are ready to sign on to a guest-worker plan that would be exponentially worse—a textbook case of hope over experience!

An even greater obstacle to a successful guest-worker program is human nature. I came across a fascinating story in the *Wall Street Journal* on a Belgian experiment to legalize prostitution that demonstrates the point. The headline: "Belgian Experiment: Make Prostitution Legal to Fight Its Ills."[32]

Does that concept sound familiar?

As you read the following excerpts, substitute "illegal aliens" for "prostitution," "illegal alien smugglers" for "human traffickers," and "coyotes" for "pimps." Let's see how "legalization" works in practice on this other form of criminal behavior.

Villa Tinto, House of Pleasure, is a pioneering example of a widening European drive to legalize prostitution, while combating the crime and violence it fosters—including the explosion in human trafficking in recent years.... By forcing the business out into the open, the governments hope to make it harder for human traffickers to thrive.[33]

Guest-worker proponents likewise claim their plan will force illegal aliens out into the open, putting smugglers and coyotes out of business. But how well does it work in practice?

But even here, human trafficking endures just outside the zone. Police say illegal prostitutes still outnumber legal ones and about a quarter of the total are the victims of human trafficking or work for pimps.[34]

And how do these illegal prostitutes manage to find work when legal ones are readily available?

Legal prostitutes typically charge more than the illegal ones—one reason the illegal ones remain in business.[35]

The article shows that in the Belgians' fight against illegal prostitution and its attendant ills, they have everything the guest-worker crowd wants: biometric screening, better working conditions, higher wages, tough enforcement (including random searches, something we'd never tolerate), increased government revenue, and workers no longer living in the shadows. Oh, I almost forgot. They also have lots and lots of *illegal prostitution.*

The fact is, guest-worker advocates can change the law, but they cannot change human nature. As legalizing prostitution has led to more prostitutes across Europe, so legalizing immigrant workers will be seen for what it is—an open invitation for more illegal immigration.

Let's look at another recent European example: amnesty in Spain. While the rest of Europe has cracked down on illegal immigration, Spain recently instituted an amnesty for illegal workers who had a job offer and could prove they'd been in the country for six months.

The plan was announced in August 2004 but was not put into effect until March 2005. Predictably, it triggered a surge of illegal immigrants into Spain from France, Italy, and Germany. At the end of the amnesty period it was estimated that there were three times more illegals in Spain than there had been a year earlier. The Spanish newspaper *El Mundo* said in an editorial: "On the horizon one can detect new avalanches of migrants—encouraged by this process—who could bring with them problems of crime and integration."[36]

The illegals will surely keep right on coming, reasonably seeing Spain as the best route to settling legally in the European Union. And why shouldn't they? There have been six amnesties in Spain since 1990. Spain's labor minister, Jesús Caldera, says there will be no more. If you were an illegal alien, would you believe him?

Not surprisingly, many illegals were reluctant to accept amnesty because they thought it might cost them their jobs. One Ecuadorian illegal told National Public Radio: "Employers don't want to pay Social Security for people who have papers, so we don't know what to do."[37] As with prostitution in Belgium, even if you offer amnesty or "legalization," large numbers will prefer to remain underground. Will Teddy Kennedy round them up?

Let me end with what one Belgian critic of legalizing prostitution said, although she could have been talking about legalizing illegal aliens:

> Critics say any benefits from legalization don't justify state-sanctioned vice. "Places like Villa Tinto are little more than assembly lines for sex where women are treated like meat for sale," says Nathalie de T'Serclaes, a Belgian senator from Brussels. She wants Belgium to embrace the Swedish model, which criminalizes clients.[38]

When it comes to illegal immigration, employers are the "clients," and going after employers is where our enforcement emphasis must be.

THE BULLWINKLE TRAP

Guest-worker supporters tell us that the linchpin to any guest-worker bill will be strict enforcement of the law. The president says, "There must be strong workplace enforcement with tough penalties for anyone, for any employer violating these laws" and that "Our goal is clear:

to return every single illegal entrant, with no exceptions." The *Arizona Republic* commends the president because he "correctly recognizes that the success of a guest-worker program also depends on enforcing laws against those who hire" illegals. [39]

Congressman Jeff Flake, a sponsor of guest-worker legislation, says, "Severe employer sanctions would be leveled against employers who hire unregistered workers."[40] Tamar Jacoby confidently asserts, "The reform package taking shape in Washington is not just going to be market-friendly—it's also going to be tough as nails."[41]

As Yogi Berra said, "It's déja vu all over again." Remember, when President Reagan signed the 1986 amnesty bill, he called tough employer sanctions the "keystone and major element" of the law.

Yet as we've already seen, the few times the federal government actually attempted to enforce the employer sanctions contained in that law, there were howls of protest, and in every case the government's efforts collapsed like a house of cards. As a result, in 2004 there wasn't a single fine levied for immigration-law violations. Zero. Zip. Zilch.

What makes anyone believe a new set of laws would be different? This skepticism is even more justified when you consider that most of those promoting a guest-worker program, including its congressional sponsors, have a history of *opposing* employer sanctions.

Take guest-worker sponsors John McCain and Jim Kolbe. When the 1986 amnesty bill was considered, both men voted against it, not because it would provide amnesty, but because the bill included employer sanctions!

The *Phoenix Gazette* reported in 1986: "'I think it's going to pass because of the added problems of drug traffic and the need to control the Mexican border,' Rep. John McCain, R-Ariz., said. 'I'm against it because of the employer sanctions.'"[42]

The *Greater Phoenix Business Journal* added: "Republican Rep. James Kolbe and Democrat Sen. Dennis DeConcini opposed the bill because of its employer sanctions and the possibility of discrimination against Hispanic citizens."[43]

And, of course, we know that Ted Kennedy opposed the 1986 amnesty because he likewise opposed employer sanctions, believing (falsely) that they would lead to discrimination against Hispanics.

So here is the deal. The president has demonstrated no inclination to enforce employer sanctions. The congressional sponsors of major guest-worker legislation have a history of opposing employer sanctions. The business community has always opposed employer sanctions because they don't think businesses should be responsible for enforcing immigration law. The liberal interest groups don't like employer sanctions because they think it will lead to discrimination against Hispanics. And what is it all these folks tell us is the key to making their grand scheme work? Employer sanctions. Can you say "oceanfront property in Arizona"?

President Bush said, "People in this debate must recognize that we will not be able to effectively enforce our immigration laws until we create a temporary-worker program." Even if you accept the dubious assumption that the federal government is capable of administering a guest-worker program, shouldn't the government first have to prove that it has the will to strictly enforce our immigration laws?

The great promise that the government will finally get tough on employers who hire illegals reminds me of the weekly routine on the old Rocky and Bullwinkle cartoon:

Bullwinkle: "Hey Rocky, watch me pull a rabbit out of my hat."
Rocky: "Again? But that trick never works."
Bullwinkle: "This time for sure!"

Poor ol' Bullwinkle never did pull a rabbit out of his hat, and my guess is that our government won't have any more inclination to enforce employer sanctions under some harebrained guest-worker plan than it does now. Until the president—any president—is willing to stand up to the corporate special interests, the identity-group grievance-mongers, and their political allies on the Right and Left, we can count on more of the same.

Strong employer enforcement is the *sine qua non* of controlling our borders and protecting our people. It could begin today without any grand new guest-worker or other immigration reform plan. But if the people don't demand it, then we might as well take the *Wall Street Journal*'s advice, open the borders, and be done with it.

CHAPTER TEN

IS OPPOSING ILLEGAL IMMIGRATION A POLITICAL LOSER FOR REPUBLICANS?

"We have six congressmen here; five are Republicans. That would not be so bad except for the kind of Republican: [Dana] Rohrabacher, [Ed] Royce; these are friends of [Tom] Tancredo, who says we need the military on the border."

—Ortiz Haro, Mexican consul in
Santa Ana, California, on Orange
County politicians

DESPITE THE HORRIBLE ATTACKS of September 11, despite the obvious nature of the threat posed by our leaky borders, and despite the polls showing the American people have had it with illegal immigration, when it comes to this undefended front in the War on Terror many of my Republican colleagues seem oblivious. Why?

Fear.

Republicans are scared of being branded as heartless, bigoted, or xenophobic. Many have become so paralyzed that they won't stand up for the rule of law, our melting pot heritage, our national security, or our low-income workers. They'll let the American people get the shaft just so they don't have to feel the heat.

That Republicans are anxious is understandable. Politics is the art of addition, not subtraction. At 14 percent of the population, Hispanics have surpassed African Americans as the largest minority group in America. Hispanics historically have voted for Democrats (although not nearly as uniformly as blacks), and many Republican political analysts and pollsters say it is just a matter of time until Republicans are demographically unable to keep their majority—unless, that is, we do whatever is necessary, including amnesty, to attract more Hispanics to our party.

The president and his chief political advisers seem to think that the way to win Hispanic votes is to coddle the business and liberal special interests by "legalizing" illegal aliens. But this is a fool's errand, because whatever the White House offers in this regard, the Democrats will *always* offer more.

When President Bush first announced his guest worker/amnesty plan, the typical response from Democrats and liberal interest groups was that it didn't go far enough. Senator Joe Lieberman said it was "too little, three years too late."[1] Former presidential candidate Dick Gephardt called it a "half measure."[2] Teddy Kennedy called it "woefully inadequate." The National Council of La Raza said it was a "bitter disappointment" and a "political ploy."[3] (My favorite response was from one illegal alien who didn't care much for the idea that he might eventually have to return to Mexico: "It's not good. The Mexican government shouldn't let him do it."[4])

Mr. President, leave the pandering to the Democrats! They have their doctorates in pandering while we keep flunking Pandering 101.

PANDER BEARS AND PANDEMONIUM

Sometimes the Democrats' pandering can reach ridiculous extremes. In 2003, at the request of far-left congresswoman Nancy Pelosi, the Phillip Burton Federal Building in San Francisco (where else!) began accepting Mexico's matrícula consular card as a valid form of identification for entering the building. Even more bizarre is the reason Pelosi made the request—she wanted cardholders to be able to visit the Internal Revenue Service office in the building. Why would illegals want to do that? To get an Individual Taxpayer Identification Number, of course, which makes it easier for them to get a mortgage and settle here permanently!

Here is the sum of Pelosi's brilliant idea: let's give illegal aliens access to a federal building in a post–September 11 world using a notoriously unreliable ID card so they can visit the IRS in furtherance of their illegal enterprise. It's a concept only a liberal could love! Sanity ultimately prevailed and the practice was stopped, but not before further erosion to the rule of law.

The Democrats' pandering runs the gamut from nutty to devious. Remember the infamous Citizenship USA program under Bill Clinton and Al Gore? Just before the 1996 elections, Gore pushed the old INS to reduce the time between filing an application and naturalization from two years to six months. The goal of the $95 million program was to make all these new citizens so thankful that they would register and vote Democrat.

But this $95 million gift to the Clinton-Gore reelection effort was fraught with fraud and abuse. Criminal background checks were rushed or forgone. According to Justice Department investigators, 180,000 immigrants did not have their fingerprints checked against criminal records. Even worse, more than 80,000 who were found to have criminal records were granted citizenship anyway![5]

Both of these examples illustrate just how far the Left will go to pander to Hispanics. Republicans can never match that, and it would be shameful if we tried—not just because it is contemptible, but also because it would suggest that we've bought into the racist Democratic assumption that Hispanics are monolithic and are all pro–illegal immigration. They're not.

Take the Protect Arizona Now (PAN, better known as Prop 200) initiative passed by Arizona voters in 2004 with a healthy 56 percent of the vote. The initiative banned illegals from receiving government services and requires presenting ID both to register and to vote. The open-borders crowd assured us that this would be a political disaster for Republicans.

Guess what? The vote didn't go quite as the critics predicted. Far from costing Hispanic votes, exit polls show that 47 percent of Arizona Hispanics voted *for* Prop 200.[6] The *Arizona Daily Star* calculated that Hispanics actually gave the initiative a "narrow majority."[7] In either case, Prop 200 did better than President Bush, who garnered 43 percent of the Arizona Hispanic vote. Fretted Mexico's foreign minister, Luis Ernesto Derbez, "It's sad and it gives an idea of how we have to work to educate even our own Mexican Americans about why it is important that these proposals are not accepted."[8] (What makes you think those "Mexican *Americans*" are yours, Señor Derbez?) Left-wing

Arizona congressman Raul Grijalva lamented, "There was no over-whelming rejection of Prop 200 in the Latino community, and we knew that going in. I wish there would have been higher opposition than it was."[9]

Republicans who think pandering on illegal immigration is the way to win Hispanic voters will be just as disappointed.

ILLEGAL IMMIGRATION? PEW!

Republicans gain Hispanic voters when we stand for economic oppor-tunity, national security, and traditional moral values. Jesse Aguila, a seventy-two-year-old Democrat from Tucson, spoke for many Hispanics when he said he voted for President Bush because of "stem cell research, abortion, marriage...issues like that." Since Hispanics also serve in the armed forces at high levels, the Republican agenda of a strong military and robust foreign policy will resonate with these voters.

Indeed, a Pew Hispanic Center poll released in August 2005 found that "Immigration is not a top concern for Latinos, even the foreign born."[10] Other issues considered more important than immigration included Social Security, moral values, and crime. Here is what previous Pew polls have found:

- 60 percent of native-born Hispanics don't believe illegal aliens should be given driver's licenses[11]
- 59 percent of Hispanics believe their children should be taught in English[12]
- 77 percent of Hispanics think abortion is unacceptable[13]
- 72 percent of Hispanics oppose homosexual sex between adults[14]

The Republican mayor of Colorado Springs, Lionel Rivera, reflects many of these views. His first act upon assuming office in 2004 was to discontinue health and family-leave benefits for same-sex partners of city employees, prompting the usual denunciations from the city's media and liberal elites. Rivera explained to Hispanic Magazine.com why he's a Republican:

Hispanic culture teaches you should be self-sufficient and take care of your family. You're Catholic and pro-life. These are things I associate with being Republican.... The Democrats address poverty with entitlements. The Republicans want to do the same thing by creating opportunity for people to go into business for themselves.[15]

On the issue of immigration in general, Pew's August 2005 poll found:

Latino public opinion overall looks favorably on immigrants. For example, clear majorities of U.S. Hispanics in several [Pew] surveys have said that unauthorized migrants help the economy by providing low-cost labor. But these views are neither unanimous nor monolithic. At least a third of the native born consistently complain that the unauthorized hurt the economy by driving down wages. Attitudes among Latinos toward options in immigration policy reflect a variety of views on immigrants and their impact on the country.[16]

Since many low-income Hispanics are in direct competition with illegal aliens for jobs, the attitude of native-born Hispanics is not surprising. It has been borne out in other polls, as we'll see below.

Perhaps most telling, however, is Pew's finding in an earlier poll that two-thirds of Hispanics who plan to become American citizens in the future do not identify themselves as either Republicans or Democrats, which means these voters are up for grabs. And whatever advantage the Democrats may have had is slipping away.

In a column just before a Democratic National Committee Hispanic summit in Texas, columnist Jaime Castillo of the *San Antonio Express-News* wrote:

The Democratic honchos might have learned more about the party's plight at my twentieth high school reunion in El Paso last week.... I was mildly surprised by what my old buddies had to say about the last presidential election. About half, I'm guessing, voted

for Bush.... The Bush backers were vocal about their support, saying they appreciated the president's strong faith in God and his firm
stand against terrorists.... [The Democrats] still must find a message that resonates with these groups that are no longer exclusively
on the liberal fringe.[17]

As we compete for Hispanic voters, let's not insult and stigmatize
them by assuming that all they care about is immigration. Most Hispanics who came here legally did so because of the opportunities this
country offers. Going forward, I hope Republicans keep in mind that
we are the party of opportunity and hard work. It is our values—not
the big-government paternalism of the Democrats—that are more in
sync with Hispanics and all immigrants, no matter where they come
from.

EVEN HILLARY GETS IT

In November 2004, Hillary Clinton told a New York radio station, "I
am, you know, adamantly against illegal immigrants.... People have to
stop employing illegal immigrants. I mean, come up to Westchester, go
to Suffolk and Nassau counties, stand on the street corners in Brooklyn or the Bronx. You're going to see loads of people waiting to get
picked up to go do yard work and construction work and domestic
work."[18]

Hillary Clinton was trying to position herself to the right of the
president on illegal immigration because she knows it's a vote-winner.
She has even introduced legislation to establish a Northern Border
Coordinator who would specifically be responsible for devising and
implementing measures to increase the security of the border between
the United States and Canada, which makes sense since New York borders Canada. And she has supported more Border Patrol agents for the
southern border.

There is not much downside for Hillary staking a position farther
to the right. This is one issue where rank-and-file Democrats are far to
the right of their leaders and even farther to the right of the liberal
special interest groups. A *Time*/CNN poll in February 2004 found that

only 28 percent of Democrats preferred a presidential nominee who "would make it easier for illegal immigrants to become citizens." A whopping 62 percent were opposed.

A May 2005 Zogby poll found that Democrats, blacks, women, and people with a household income below $75,000 were the segments of the population most opposed to illegal immigration. It is easy to see why. Unlike the editorial writers at the *Wall Street Journal*, they are the ones most likely to be in direct competition with illegals for jobs.

To be sure, Hillary's toughness on illegal immigration is for the most part rhetorical. She opposed the REAL ID act; her idea of fighting illegal immigration is amnesty; she supports in-state tuition for illegals; and she opposed the Bush administration's proposal to require passports at U.S. borders.

Hillary's tough talk on illegal immigration gets a pass from the left-wing groups because they know where she really stands. In fact, in a July 2005 speech Hillary gave before the radically pro–illegal alien National Council of La Raza, the issue of illegal immigration never came up! Can you imagine a Republican ever getting away with something like that?

When you combine her rhetoric on illegal immigration with her efforts to reach out to abortion foes by saying, among other things, that abortion is "a sad, even tragic choice to many, many women," it is clear that Hillary is trying to position herself as a cultural centrist for 2008. She's not the only Democrat who understands the political appeal of reaching out to the Right.

In August 2005, New Mexico governor Bill Richardson declared a state of emergency in four counties along the U.S.-Mexico border. A liberal Democrat with national ambitions, Richardson promised local officials $1.5 million in aid to deal with what he called "a chaotic situation" involving illegal-alien smuggling, drug smuggling, and murder. He criticized the federal government for not doing its job, telling Norah O'Donnell on *Hardball*, "We're taking matters into our own hands!"[19] (He sounds like a vigilante, doesn't he?) He even called the Minutemen "patriots." (Now I know he's a vigilante!)

Sounds like the governor is our kind of guy, right? Not so fast.

Richardson is not part of the solution—he is part of the problem. He unapologetically offers illegal aliens driver's licenses and in-state tuition. He greeted the 2003 Immigration Workers' Freedom Ride Rally (organized to push for amnesty for illegals) by saying, "Viva la raza! Vivan los immigrantes! Bienvenidos immigrantes! Thank you for coming to Santa Fe. Know that New Mexico is your home. We will protect you. You have rights here."[20]

His "state of emergency" is nothing but more political grandstanding from a soft-on-illegal immigration Democrat trying to establish some bona fides on the issue. Hillary, Richardson, and the like ought to start their own "Rhetoric Over Reality" caucus.

IF THE MEXICANS GET IT, WHY CAN'T REPUBLICANS?

Even the Mexicans have figured out that political trouble awaits those who are unwilling to acknowledge the problem of illegal immigration. A perfect example is the situation we have in Arizona with Democratic governor Janet Napolitano. She, like Richardson, has national ambitions, and is a shrewd and calculating politician—a far-left liberal who talks like a centrist (she learned well from Bill Clinton). Within days of Governor Richardson declaring a state of emergency along New Mexico's border, Napolitano did so as well, condemning the Bush administration for not doing more to stop the violence on the border.

While she likes to talk tough about the crisis on the border and *loves* to point the finger of blame at federal officials in Washington for everything that goes wrong in Arizona, her actions betray her as someone who is genuinely sympathetic to illegal immigration. As governor, she has vetoed legislation that would:

- require proof of citizenship to register to vote
- expand the range of benefits denied to illegal aliens under Prop 200
- authorize police to investigate, arrest, detain, or deport illegal aliens

- prohibit illegal immigrants from attending college or being classified as in-state residents for tuition purposes
- declare English the official state language
- ban state and local governments from accepting matrícula consular cards issued by the government of Mexico and other foreign forms of identification

Do you detect a pattern here?

Napolitano also once promised to sign legislation to grant driver's licenses to illegal aliens, although she has tried mightily to back away from that position. When I wrote to the governor asking her to renounce it, she responded:

> I have not asked the state legislature to permit undocumented individuals to apply for driver's licenses, nor do I intend to do so. I have said, IF the Arizona legislature were to pass such a bill, I would probably sign it. They are not likely to pass such a measure. This was stated in response to a hypothetical question.
>
> Rather than focusing on this nonexistent circumstance, I believe it would be better for our state to generate more energy on substantive border issues that would have a real impact on our situation; i.e., ensuring that Arizona receives appropriate federal funding to protect our border.

Her idea of a "substantive border issue" that will have "a real impact"? A blatantly political stunt: send invoices to the federal government for the costs of illegal immigration picked up by the state of Arizona—invoices that Napolitano knows will never be paid. In March 2005 Napolitano sent a bill for $195.6 million to the Justice Department to recover the cost to Arizona of jailing these criminals in 2003, 2004, and part of 2005.

Do you think those invoices would have been sent if a Democrat occupied the White House? I don't either.

Next she declared a state of emergency in the four Arizona counties bordering Mexico because of the crime and smuggling activity—but *didn't call out the National Guard!* How many times has a governor anywhere in the country declared a state of emergency on a security matter without calling out the Guard?

Napolitano's record of being soft on, if not outright supportive of, illegal immigration has not gone unnoticed or unappreciated south of the border. In March 2004, seven Mexican senators visited Arizona to investigate the effects of Prop 200. For three days they met with Arizona political and community leaders. Upon their return to Mexico, the seven wrote a scathing report, calling Arizona a "desolate panorama"[21] of rising anti-immigrant sentiment. According to the *Arizona Republic*, one delegation member stated: "The anti-Mexican climate in the state of Arizona is undeniable. The anti-Mexican atmosphere that prevails there, far from diminishing, is being felt with ever-increasing force."[22]

While there is no denying that Arizonans have had it with illegal immigration, the claim of rampant anti-Mexican discrimination is ludicrous on its face. As we've seen, about half of the Hispanics in Arizona—the vast majority of Mexican ancestry—voted *for* Prop 200. Are they all anti-Mexican?

But the most mind-boggling aspect of their visit is that they did not even request a meeting with Napolitano. Do you want to know why? You won't believe it: "The [Mexican] consul made it very clear that the political circumstances of Arizona, and especially of the governor, are currently difficult in light of the elections [in 2006]. The Mexican legislators judged it pertinent not to ask for an appointment with her, because her political position should be handled with care."[23]

The report went on to call Napolitano "a true ally in the fight in favor of our migrants."[24] Take a look at her record outlined above and it is easy to see why.

Arizona is on the front line of the illegal immigration invasion of our country and from the Mexican point of view, our governor is an ally in *their* cause. To me it is real simple: if you are a "true ally" of illegal immigrants, you cannot be a "true ally" of our national security, our low-wage American workers, our melting pot heritage, or our rule of law.

These Mexican senators have figured out that in America it is not good politics to be seen as sympathetic to illegal immigration. So why is it that so many Republicans remain so clueless?

HOW TO WIN HISPANIC VOTES—DO WHAT'S RIGHT!

Maybe part of the problem is that Republicans are so easily spooked. In April 2005 two pro–illegal alien groups, the American Immigration Lawyers Association (AILA) and the National Immigration Forum (NIF), commissioned a poll that had many Republicans ready to surrender to a guest worker/amnesty plan. Respected Republican pollster Ed Goeas and Democratic pollster Celinda Lake conducted the poll, which created quite a buzz on Capitol Hill. According to the AILA, the poll revealed that

> American voters support a system that combines toughness with fairness, and provides a path to citizenship with reasonable requirements, implements an effective guest-worker program, and reunites families. Voters want a system that rewards immigrants who come here to work hard, pay taxes, and learn English.[25]

I have been over the entire poll and it shows nothing of the kind. In fact, the poll is an exercise in pro-illegal propaganda—the questions are rigged to generate a predetermined outcome. It is known in the business as a "push poll" because it pushes respondents in the direction the pollster wants to take them. The only thing this "poll" shows is just how politically correct and desperate the AILA and NIF really are.

This was supposed to be a poll on immigration policy, yet the terms "illegal alien" and "illegal immigrant" appear nowhere. There are only "temporary workers" and "undocumented workers." And, hey, what are a few documents among friends? The questions describe the preferred immigration proposals as "bipartisan," a word that any pollster will tell you is worth several extra points. The tricks go on and on.

One of the more cynical attempts at spin I've seen came from the Manhattan Institute's Tamar Jacoby, a supposed conservative no less.

Although the entire guest-worker effort is driven by ethnic identity politics, she claims that those of us pushing enforcement are "focused more on politics" while those pushing guest worker/amnesty plans are "focused on governing."[26] The *Arizona Republic* goes even further, claiming that a guest-worker program is "courageous" while enforcement is "the easy way out."[27] Of course, the opposite is the case. Truly enforcing our immigration laws would require the federal government to do difficult and uncomfortable things that will get certain special interests very angry. Enforcement is not for the fainthearted.

In contrast, a guest-worker scheme is based on the same defeatist notion—we can't stop it so we may as well legalize it—used by proponents of legalizing drugs and prostitution. It is not courageous; it is *surrender*. It's also a convenient way for the government to grant *itself* amnesty for decades of looking the other way while the rule of law was ground underfoot by a human stampede.

Guest-worker advocates know that they are losing the debate and are resorting to more desperate and more absurd arguments, and we can expect more of this kind of twaddle as this debate heats up. The open-borders crowd simply has no compelling arguments. All they offer are linguistic obfuscation and the race card. We must not let them control the language, because if they control the language, they control the debate.

According to conservative economist and pundit Stephen Moore, the *Wall Street Journal*, and others on the pro-amnesty Right, being tough on illegal immigration is not a winning political issue. They offer as proof the failed primary challenges in 2004 to congressmen Jim Kolbe and Jeff Flake, both friends and Republican colleagues from Arizona. Though both their opponents made immigration a major issue, Kolbe and Flake won with 57 and 59 percent of the vote respectively. The *Journal* asserts the two "prevailed easily" and that "the message is that anti-immigrant populism may look good in some polls but it doesn't work come Election Day."[28]

All it really shows is how difficult it is to beat an incumbent, especially in a primary. I also had a primary opponent in 2004 (a pro-abortion single-issue candidate), and I won by 80 to 20 percent. I can tell you there is no way I would have considered my race "easy" if I had won with just 57 or 59 percent. The fact that these two popular incumbents drew primary challenges because of their position on immigration is far more telling than the final outcome.

Further, consider the candidacy of James Gilchrist in California. Gilchrist is one of the founders of the Minuteman Project and a political novice who ran as an American Independent Party candidate in the special congressional election to fill the seat vacated by Republican congressman Chris Cox. After the October primary, the race had shaped up as a two-man affair between Gilchrist and the Republican candidate, John Campbell. The *Los Angeles Times* reported: "'This is the first time I've seen a third-party candidate with such a strong showing,' marveled political consultant Scott Hart....'Illegal immigration was Gilchrist's issue and his platform, and that's why people were voting for him. It shows how strong the issue is.'"[29]

Poet Charles Péguy once said, "We will never know how many acts of cowardice have been motivated by the fear of appearing not sufficiently progressive." He could have been talking about the debate on illegal immigration. But my Republican colleagues need to get over their fear of being "not sufficiently progressive." Hispanics, like most other Americans, will respond to our agenda of less government, lower taxes, a strong national defense, and personal responsibility. I know it can be done.

My former district was home to seven different Indian tribes and Native Americans made up about a quarter of the population, making them by far the largest minority group. The tribes had a long history of voting for Democrats. I set out to change that—and I did, building my vote among Native Americans every two years. In fact, I was so effective that when new congressional lines were being drawn after the 2000 census, tribes were asking the redistricting commission to be drawn into my new district.

How did I do it? Instead of pandering to the tribes, I set out to convince them that they had more in common with Republicans than they ever imagined. I listened to their concerns and offered conservative policies to meet them. I never abandoned my principles or told tribal leaders something just because I thought it was what they or their people wanted to hear. I didn't, and don't, agree with the tribes on every issue, but when we do agree they know I'll fight hard for them. As a result, a columnist in *Indian Country Today* once said that John McCain and I were the two best friends Native Americans had in the entire Congress. Not bad for a guy who started out with just 15 percent of the Native American vote!

If there is one thing I've learned in politics, it's that you will seldom regret it if you do what you think is right and in the best interests of the country, regardless of the political risks. I believe enforcing our laws against illegal immigration is the right thing to do—and I believe the American people, including Hispanic Americans, agree with me.

CHAPTER ELEVEN

WHAT TO DO ABOUT ILLEGAL IMMIGRATION

"What strikes me funny is when something is illegal, it's illegal. Enforce the law. I wish it was more complicated than that. But that's the way I do with my city and it works out fine."[1]

—Sonny Bono on illegal immigration

AS YOU CAN TELL FROM THE ABOVE QUOTE, Sonny Bono was truly a man ahead of his time. Enforce the law. Now there's a novel concept!

Besides its simplicity, enforcing the law also has something else going for it—we know it works. If we put our minds to it, we can stop illegal immigration and even induce illegals to return home.

Yet the amnesty-first crowd pointedly ignores this evidence and continues to insist that enforcement doesn't work. But the alternative to enforcement is open borders and the continued erosion of respect for the rule of law in the United States.

Furthermore, our approach to immigration enforcement has been schizophrenic. We spend billions to guard our borders, but if you make it across, it's "Welcome to America, can we sell you a mortgage?" As one retired cop asked: "Who came up with the idea of feds not arresting illegals? The feds need to get back to basics. If you're an illegal, you go to jail, no matter where you are. It's that simple."[2]

Unfortunately, it doesn't work that way. Too many government agencies and other public institutions work at cross-purposes. Illegal immigration threatens to overwhelm our country and it is a threat to our national security. We need action now. We can no longer tolerate federal agencies that offer illegal immigrants the rights of citizens and legal residents.

We can no longer tolerate federal agencies that beg off enforcing immigration laws because "it's not our job."

We can no longer tolerate liberal police chiefs who refuse to enforce immigration laws. We can no longer tolerate state governments that issue driver's licenses to illegal aliens or grant them public benefits and in-state tuition.

We can no longer tolerate greedy corporations accepting the matrícula consular card or catering to illegals so they can make a few extra bucks.

We can no longer tolerate hospitals refusing the simple task of asking patients about their immigration status and then asking to be reimbursed by the federal government for the care they provide illegal aliens.

Congress has made a start. We've created the Department of Homeland Security and separated the immigration enforcement and citizenship functions. We've funded 500 new Border Patrol agents, 170 interior investigators, 114 detention officers, and 1,360 more detention beds. We've reformed our asylum laws so that terrorists can no longer falsely claim persecution. We've told states that if they don't require proof of lawful presence in the United States before issuing a driver's license, their licenses will not be recognized as legitimate ID by the federal government (which means they could not be used to board a plane, for instance). And we've ensured the completion of the San Diego border fence in a timely fashion. But much more needs to be done.

The American people, as usual, get it. Polls show that they are fed up with illegal immigration and want something done about it. A May 2005 Zogby poll found that 76 percent of Americans don't think the government is doing enough to stop illegal immigration. A CBS poll done six months later came up with a nearly identical result (75 percent). Americans are so disgusted that a strong majority in the Zogby poll said they want troops deployed on the border as a temporary measure to stop illegal crossings.

Of course, any concerted effort to strengthen and enforce our immigration laws is met with howls of protest by the politically correct elites. Instead of taking action, they lecture us about the "complexities" of the problem and the "realities on the ground." They accuse us of bigotry and discrimination because we worry about the effect illegal immigration is having on our diversity and our melting pot heritage. They tell us we need these workers to do jobs Americans won't. And they downplay the national security threat, calling it a diversion. This is one member of Congress who has had enough.

At its root, the problem is simply one of illicit supply and illicit demand. We have focused most of our energy (though not nearly enough resources) on the supply side of the problem, in other words, on stopping illegal border crossings, and not nearly enough on the demand side, the businesses that are addicted to cheap illegal labor. To get control of illegal immigration we need both tougher border security to keep new illegals from coming here and tougher interior enforcement based on "broken windows" policing to induce illegals already here to return home. Let's be clear: we do not need nor do we want "round-ups" of illegal immigrants. The problem is decades old and can't be solved overnight. But a long-term strategy based on attrition can be successful.

As we consider ways to stop illegal immigration, we should be guided by two overriding principles:

1. We must not reward lawbreakers, including illegal aliens or those who hire them.
2. We must not create incentives for even more illegal immigration.

Just about every plan now being considered in Congress violates one or both of these principles. That is especially true of a guest-worker scheme, which also has something else going against it—history. There has never been a successful guest-worker program—not here, not in Europe, not anywhere. France, Germany, and Switzerland are still dealing with problems generated by guest-worker plans from decades ago. Meanwhile,

Saudi Arabia's six million guest workers struggle to survive under conditions that have been called "modern-day slavery." And if our bracero programs were so successful, why don't we have one now? (Answer: they lowered wages for American workers and increased illegal immigration.)

A guest-worker plan is exactly the wrong approach to this problem. There's a better way.

BORDER ENFORCEMENT: TROOPS ON THE BORDER NOW

In an earlier chapter, we saw how illegal border crossers are destroying private property all along the Mexican border. What do you think would happen if President Bush's Texas ranch were on the border with Mexico instead of hundreds of miles away? Do you think illegal aliens, smugglers, and drug dealers would dare to challenge the president's security force, tear down his fences, wander around his property, steal his pickup truck, or come into his home demanding food, water, and a change of clothes?

They wouldn't if they were sane. By the same token, no American deserves to have his or her property overrun by criminals as their government stands by and does nothing.

Ronald Reagan once observed, "This country has lost control of its borders, and no country can sustain that kind of position."[3] Thus the obvious place to begin stopping illegal immigration is at the border—particularly our southern border with Mexico. To be sure, the Canadian border and official ports of entry are also concerns, but we simply cannot ignore the central reality that most illegal immigrants come here across our southern border. It is time to start treating that border as the security threat it is.

We need boots on the ground to make the border a real barrier. Ten thousand new Border Patrol agents have been authorized by Congress. It's time to get them funded, hired, trained, properly equipped, and on the border. And we need to give them unmanned aerial vehicles, camera poles, radar, vehicle barriers, ground sensors, and the tools they lack but that are necessary to do the job effectively. I have seen many demonstrations of these technologies and I know they work.

At the Barry M. Goldwater Range near Yuma, Arizona, the Marines are using a specially designed ground surveillance system that tracks movement and pinpoints locations of vehicles and people, saving lives and dollars. When the Marines spot something on the range, they relay Global Positioning System coordinates to Border Patrol agents who go out and do their job. It has been hugely successful. Captain Terry Johnson with the Provost Marshal's Office at the Yuma Marine Corps Air Station said of the system, "This is the twenty-first-century way for the military to do what we've been doing for a hundred years. Before we did it with fences and signs, 'restricted area, stay out.' Because we have such wide areas here in Yuma, doing signs and fences really isn't a realistic thing to do with miles and miles of area."[4]

If we applied the appropriate technologies for the various terrains all along the border, agents could be even more efficient and effective.

My plan would also authorize the secretary of defense to assign members of the Army, Navy, Air Force, and Marine Corps to assist the Department of Homeland Security in the performance of border protection functions. I'm not talking about a permanent deployment, but a temporary one to stabilize the situation, after which troops could be redeployed as required. This is not a radical suggestion. Indeed, one Zogby poll showed a majority (53 percent) of Americans want troops deployed on the border as a temporary measure to stop illegal crossings.

This is not a recommendation I make lightly. For almost my entire public career I resisted the notion of putting troops along our border, even twice voting that way in the House. But September 11 and the growing border violence have changed my mind—along with the recent admission by the secretary of the Department of Homeland Security that it will take *five years* to gain operational control of our borders.

Visit the border enough and you soon notice that almost everyone who lives there is armed, mostly for protection from illegals. In a situation so volatile and potentially lethal, the alien smugglers and drug traffickers must never outman or outgun the good guys. And if I were the governor of Arizona, New Mexico, Texas, or California, I would not hesitate to station National Guard units along the border.

I know our troops are spread thin due to the fighting in Iraq, Afghanistan, and other deployments around the world. But our border has become a front in the War on Terror. The Minutemen reduced illegal crossings to a trickle just by sitting in lawn chairs with binoculars—imagine what trained troops could do.

Since the Posse Comitatus Act bars the military from enforcing domestic laws without congressional authorization, stationing troops on the border will require an act of Congress. (National Guard troops are not subject to Posse Comitatus unless they are federalized, so governors could use them for border-related duties without any change to the law.) Last year, Republican congressman Virgil Goode of Virginia offered an amendment that would authorize troops on the border. It passed by 245 to 184, but the Senate killed it, as it has done before. The Senate will keep killing it until the American people demand that it pass.

In his speech from New Orleans after Hurricane Katrina, President Bush said, "It is now clear that a challenge on this scale requires greater federal authority and a broader role for the armed forces." The *Wall Street Journal* editorialized that "the New Orleans mess improved only after the Pentagon got involved."[5]

Of course, the *Journal* would never support deploying troops along the border to stop illegal immigration because it believes in open borders. But I say we have a "Category 5" illegal immigration problem, and if deploying troops is good enough for dealing with a hurricane, then it is surely good enough to deal with an issue that has far greater national security implications.

As a last resort, we should also consider building a border security fence from the Pacific Ocean to the Gulf of Mexico, with at least twenty-five ports of entry along the way. The cost of a modern border security fence is estimated at four to eight billion dollars—a bargain when you consider what illegal immigration is costing our country.

Some on the Left have ridiculed the idea, saying that it would amount to building our own Berlin Wall. That is nonsense. The Berlin Wall kept people prisoner; a security fence along our border would keep people from entering illegally. It's the difference between prison bars and the bars that people put over their windows to guard against burglars. A border fence would have more in common with the fence the Israelis have built, which has been so successful in keeping out terrorists.

Despite overwhelming evidence to the contrary, sympathizers of illegal immigration continue to claim that sealing the border is not feasible. They are wrong. Not only can we do it, we *must* do it. Additionally, if we remove the incentive to cross the border by toughening interior and workplace enforcement, we can eventually, as one of the Minutemen quipped, put the "bored" back in Border Patrol. But first we need to put the "order" back in border.

INTERIOR ENFORCEMENT: THE KEY TO SUCCESS

What is it that causes millions to leave their homeland to come to the United States illegally? For most, it is just one thing: work. Illegal aliens are not coming here to escape political persecution or for religious freedom or because they long to become Americans; they are coming here to either get a job or to be with a family member who has one.

The demand for cheap labor is the magnet drawing illegal aliens into our country. If we get serious about punishing the businesses that hire illegal aliens, they will stop hiring them. And with no prospect of a job, illegal aliens will stop coming and, just as important, many of those already here will return home.

Here is what we need to do about employment.

- Create a tamper-proof Social Security card with an embedded photograph that says the holder has the right to work in the United States. No match, no job, no exceptions. While the new Social Security card is phased in (you would only need to get the new card the first time you switch jobs), the Basic Pilot verification system should be made mandatory for every business and every new hire.
- The 2,900 interior enforcement agents we have now are just not enough. We should add 10,000 new personnel whose sole responsibility would be enforcing employer compliance, 250 additional immigration judges, and 500 Department of

Homeland Security trial attorneys. To ensure that they can get the job done, we should authorize $100 million per year to prosecute those who hire illegal aliens.

- The current penalties for hiring illegal aliens are not severe enough to act as a deterrent. For companies with an established pattern of hiring illegal workers, we should increase the fine from $10,000 to $50,000 per illegal hired, and the jail term to one year per illegal alien hired up to a maximum of five.

I firmly believe that the sight of a CEO on television doing a perp walk after getting busted for hiring illegal aliens would have a greater impact on illegal immigration than hiring a thousand Border Patrol agents.

GET THE SSA AND THE IRS OFF THE SIDELINES AND INTO THE GAME

Earlier we saw how the Social Security Administration and the Internal Revenue Service actually enable illegal immigration. I have introduced legislation to make the SSA and IRS full partners in protecting our homeland and in protecting the integrity of their own documents.

Under my plan, whenever the SSA informs an employer via a "no-match" letter that the Social Security number being used by an illegal is no good, the SSA will send a copy of that letter to the Department of Homeland Security. The illegal will also get a "no-match letter" telling him that the information is being shared with DHS.

Between Basic Pilot and SSA's own verification system, there is no excuse for businesses hiring employees with phony Social Security numbers and then filing bad W-2s with the IRS. If employers file W-2s with a bad SSN, the IRS should hit them with a fine unless the error was an honest mistake. In addition, we should increase the fines for submitting false W-2 data from $50 to $500 per incident, and raise the overall maximum from $250,000 to $2,500,000.

Illegal aliens are abusing the IRS's Individual Taxpayer Identification Numbers to get bank loans and other financial services. The IRS has informed my office that it is likely the bulk of tax returns submitted with a U.S. address and an ITIN only (no Social Security number)

are filed by people who are in the U.S. illegally. The IRS should therefore be required to provide the Department of Homeland Security
with a list of the names and mailing addresses of all those assigned an
ITIN. And the IRS should provide Congress with an annual listing of
businesses with the greatest number and highest percentage of bad
Social Security numbers. Today, publicizing such lists is against the
law. I know because I tried to get them. But Americans have the right
to know which companies are taking advantage of loopholes to
exploit illegal workers.

Finally, in order to safeguard the future solvency of the Social Security system, the president must not complete the totalization agreement his administration has signed with Mexico.

ON CRIME THE SOLUTION IS CLEAR

Our country is suffering from an epidemic of illegal immigrant crime.
The CLEAR Act introduced by Republican congressman Charlie Norwood of Georgia could help undo some of the damage.

CLEAR stands for the Clear Law Enforcement for Criminal Alien
Removal Act. While it may be one of the most tortured bill names in
history (some folks in Washington will do anything for a good
acronym), this bill lives up to its name. It is a clear, commonsense
response to illegal alien crime—and it drives the liberals crazy.

CLEAR would enlist the nation's 700,000 local and state police officers to assist the outmanned 2,900 federal agents now struggling—and
failing—to enforce our nation's immigration laws. CLEAR is not about
"round-ups" of illegal aliens, as some on the Left disingenuously claim,
but focuses on apprehending the 465,000 illegal aliens with deportation orders who have gone missing. Of this number, 84,000 are convicted criminals and 3,800 of these are from countries with a known al
Qaeda presence. Police would be asked to assist in apprehending these
fugitives in the normal course of their duties. Here are two examples of
the kinds of criminals that CLEAR aims to capture.

- In a June 2005 operation across New England, 187 illegal
  immigrants were arrested. Most had outstanding deportation

orders for violent crimes, including assault and battery, rape, and arson. Again, most had spent time in jail and were then released instead of being deported as they should have been.[6]

- In October 2003, immigration authorities in New York City apprehended fifty-six foreign nationals who had been convicted of sex crimes against children. All fifty-six had served their sentences and were supposed to have been deported, but were released back into the community because of the gaping holes in our immigration system.[7]

Let me tell you about some of those who were among the fifty-six captured in New York City. There was a Salvadoran man who raped his ten-year-old niece; another Salvadoran man who sexually assaulted a six-year-old boy; a Trinidad native who raped his seven-year-old niece; and an Ecuadorian man who sexually assaulted a two-year-old. These are vicious criminals who should never find safe harbor in America.

Sixteen targets of the New York City sweep were not caught and may never be because their names, felonious histories, and deportation status are not in the National Crime Information Center (NCIC) database accessed by law enforcement across the country. If these illegal alien criminals were pulled over for a traffic violation in, say, Phoenix, the police would not know that they are convicted sex offenders wanted for deportation.

Under CLEAR, however, their names would appear in the NCIC along with the standing deportation order. Local police could then hold them for federal authorities. The bill also provides a billion dollars for equipment, training, and detention facilities for police departments that cooperate with federal authorities; it denies federal payments for incarcerating illegal aliens if they don't. Cities with sanctuary policies would *not* qualify for assistance.

When illegals brazenly pose for a picture in *BusinessWeek* or identify themselves in newspaper stories, many Americans ask me why they aren't immediately picked up and deported. They should be. But the Achilles' heel of our immigration policy is that illegal immigrants know we aren't serious about enforcing our own laws.

We need to implement a "broken windows" approach to immigration enforcement by punishing minor as well as major infractions. I see this concept at work every day on a Capitol Hill street corner where one particular police officer strictly enforces the ordinance against jaywalking. As a result, you rarely see anyone attempt it. Illegal immigrants and potential border crossers need that same kind of conditioning.

CATCH AND DEPORT

U.S. immigration policy, as I have documented, is rife with infuriating contradictions, failures, and abuses of common sense. Few, if any, surpass the idiotic and indefensible practice known as "catch and release." It is disgraceful that the federal government would condone this idiotic policy that allows thousands of illegal aliens to be caught and released each year.

Additionally, our borders have become only a minor inconvenience for illegal alien trespassers; so have the exit terms of our visas and even our deportation orders. Even worse, illegal aliens use our own laws to assist them in their illegal endeavor—such as when OTMs come across the Mexican border and turn themselves in to the Border Patrol. What a deal for the illegals, and what a mockery of the rule of law.

There are some 2.5 to 3 million aliens illegally present in the United States because they overstayed their visas, and another 125,000 to 150,000 join them every year. The threat this poses to our homeland security becomes clear when you recall that five of the September 11 terrorists violated the terms of their visas at one time or another.

Given the enormity and unacceptable risks associated with this problem, we must address the inadequacy of our obsolete tracking systems and our lax interior visa enforcement. While the US-VISIT program (see Chapter One) has done well in preventing criminals and terrorists from getting into our country, immigration authorities don't have the manpower to go after visa overstayers. We may need to eventually get the private sector involved as a force multiplier by requiring applicants for nonimmigrant visas to post a visa term compliance bond as a condition of entering the country. If the alien skips out on the terms of his or her visa, the bail agent would be free to track down and deliver the alien to immigration authorities.

But once we catch illegals we need a place to put them. Immigration officials should never be in the position of having to release an illegal alien back onto the streets because of a lack of detention space. Currently, there are 20,000 beds available for detaining illegal immigrants. Congress authorized an additional 40,000 in the 9-11 Commission implementation bill, but never provided the money for them. We need to pass the funding now. Also, since we are in another round of military base closings, why not look to turn some of those facilities into illegal alien detention centers?

Additionally, immigration authorities are testing electronic bracelets and voice recognition systems to keep track of illegal aliens pending deportation. These programs should be expanded.

We can no longer tolerate serious criminal aliens being let loose onto America's streets after they have served time in prison. If the government were doing its job properly, the New York City raid cited previously should not have been necessary. We must develop a system to identify illegal aliens while they are still in jail so that they can be deported upon completion of their sentences. If federal agents aren't available to take the criminal aliens into custody, state and local law enforcement should be allowed to keep them in jail—at federal expense—until a transfer can be made.

Finally, we need to do something about countries that refuse to accept the repatriation of their citizens. The Supreme Court recently ruled that deportable aliens may only be held for six months. If their home country won't take them back, they must be set free—even if they have a criminal history. Congress needs to enact legislation to give the Department of Homeland Security the authorization to detain aliens for as long as it takes to deport them. In turn, we need to tell countries that dump these illegals on America's doorstep that their citizens will be refused admission to the United States until they agree to accept these deported criminals.

ANCHORS AWAY

Anchor babies—or babies born to illegal aliens in the U.S.—are one of the most vexing problems we face with illegal immigration. Since all babies born in this country are considered American citizens, anchor babies qualify for welfare, subsidized housing, Medicaid, and other public assistance—assistance that benefits the illegal parents as well as the child. With an estimated 300,000 to 350,000 anchor babies born every year,[8] the costs are astronomical.

In time, anchor babies begin a chain of *legal* immigration (or amnesty on the installment plan) that will allow just a few countries to unfairly dominate legal immigration well into the future. And of course, like everything else in this debate, once the lawyers get involved things get very strange very quickly—like the time lawyers for a pregnant Mexican woman who had been deported argued that she should be readmitted because under federal law her fetus was eligible for citizenship.

The United States is one of the few countries in the world that still grants what is known as birthright citizenship. We do so because of a misinterpretation of the Fourteenth Amendment to the Constitution, which states, "All persons born or naturalized in the United States, and subject to the jurisdiction thereof, are citizens of the United States."

A strong argument can be made that the Fourteenth Amendment was never meant to bestow citizenship on children born to foreigners in this country. Indeed, the author of the citizenship clause, Senator Jacob Howard, made clear what he had in mind:

> Every person born within the limits of the United States, and subject to their jurisdictions, is by virtue of natural laws and national law a citizen of the United States. This will not, of course, include persons born in the United States who are foreigners, aliens, who belong to the families of ambassadors or foreign ministers accredited to the Government of the United States, but will include every other class of persons.[9]

The implication for children born to illegal immigrants is clear. As lawyer Madeleine Cosman puts it:

The Constitution grants citizenship to all persons born or natural-ized in the United States and "subject to the jurisdiction thereof." An illegal alien mother is subject to the jurisdiction of her country. The baby of an illegal alien mother also is subject to that home country's jurisdiction.[10]

And ask yourself, if the true intent of the Fourteenth Amendment was to bestow birthright citizenship on anyone born in the United States, why did Senator Howard bother with the "subject to the juris-diction thereof" clause?

I believe that it is time for Congress to put an end to blanket birthright citizenship. Republican congressman Nathan Deal of Geor-gia has introduced legislation that would grant automatic citizenship to children born in the United States only when at least one parent is a citizen (in the case of illegitimate births, the mother must be a citizen) or a legal permanent resident. While this seems like common sense, the usual left-wing illegal-immigrant advocates have vilified it. Leo Chavez, a professor of anthropology at the University of California–Irvine, told CNN's Lou Dobbs: "And, you know, basically, it's really un-American . . . in this country we don't punish the children for the sins of their parents, and that's exactly what this law does."[11]

We hear the "sins of their parents" argument a lot, usually from those who don't really believe the parents have committed any sins to begin with!

But by granting automatic citizenship to children of illegal aliens born here, we are *rewarding* children for the sins of their parents. We're rewarding the parents too, who indirectly reap the benefits of one of the most valuable commodities on earth—American citizen-ship.

Birthright citizenship is another government giveaway that is just too expensive and detrimental to tolerate. It's time to end it.

ENGLISH: THE LANGUAGE OF SUCCESS

At a press conference a few weeks after the London terrorist bombings, British prime minister Tony Blair made this cogent observation that gets to the heart of a debate we are having in this country: "You've got people who may be here, you know, sometimes twenty years or more and who still don't speak English. That worries me. I mean, it worries me, because I think there's a separateness there that may be unhealthy."[12]

It is just as unhealthy on this side of the pond.

As we know, the *sine qua non* of immigrant assimilation in America is, at minimum, learning to speak and understand English fluently. English is not only required to excel in school, but it is also necessary for economic success. Indeed, non-proficiency in English is the single largest factor explaining why Hispanic children don't perform as well in school as other immigrant groups.

That's why I support making English—the language of our Constitution—the official language of our nation. We should abolish bilingual education. And we should make English proficiency and a thorough knowledge of American civics non-negotiable requirements for immigrants to acquire citizenship.

Back in 1986, the *Wall Street Journal* editorialized: "Some [activists] think legislation is needed to make English an official language, though surely the growth of English as an international language is likely to make such parochial laws unnecessary."[13]

That cocksure prediction looks ridiculous now. While English usage has continued to grow outside our borders, in many parts of America it is in headlong retreat. Hispanics living in Phoenix, Los Angeles, Chicago, Miami, and many other places can pretty much live day-to-day speaking only Spanish. Non-Spanish-speaking immigrants, for the most part, do not have that luxury.

We know from our earlier experience that Italians only really assimilated once Italian immigration stopped and there were no new immigrants to reinforce the cultural and linguistic connection to "the old country." Just the opposite is happening today. The constant flow of Spanish-speaking illegal immigrants across our border ensures that in many areas Spanish will continue to compete with English—to the detriment of Hispanic children and their future.

The Left will have none of this. They oppose English as the official language because...well, because they really don't like America very much and equate Americanization with cultural oppression. They reject the very notion that there is a uniquely American identity, or that, if there is one, it is superior to any other. They see America strictly in terms of ethnic identity; a place where group membership trumps all else. So they push bilingual education, racial quotas, and ethnic studies. As I said earlier, they don't want America to change immigrants; they want immigrants to change America—and not for the better.

Political theorist Michael Walzer went so far as to say, "A radical program of Americanization would really be un-American. It isn't inconceivable that America will one day become an American nation-state, the many giving way to the one, but that is not what it is now; nor is that its destiny. America has no singular national destiny—and to be an 'American' is, finally, to know that and to be more or less content with it."[14]

There you have it: Americanization is un-American!

Americans have to decide which vision of America they want. Are we going to be the melting pot or the tossed salad?

Of course, families should be free—even encouraged—to speak their native tongues in their own home and to celebrate their heritage. But a complex modern society like ours—with sophisticated democratic institutions requiring a high degree of civic participation—demands a common language, and in the United States that language must be English. And if an official language is good enough for Mexico, it should be good enough for us.

DENY IN-STATE TUITION TO ILLEGAL ALIENS

The cost of educating the millions of illegal alien children and U.S.-born children of illegal aliens runs to almost $29 billion annually. In a transparent bid for Hispanic votes, many politicians want to provide even more educational benefits to illegal aliens by allowing them to pay in-state tuition at state universities. If they had their way, illegal aliens would not only pay lower tuition than foreign students legally here on student visas, but also less than out-of-state Americans. Even worse, for every illegal alien given a space at a state university, a legal student might be left out in the cold.

Aside from rewarding illegal behavior, in-state tuition for illegals also amounts to de facto amnesty. After all, if our government won't deny illegal aliens a subsidized college education, what makes anyone think our government will deny them a job once they finish school?

Proponents argue that refusing them in-state tuition is punishing illegal kids for the sins of their parents. But every time a university admission goes to an illegal alien over an American, the American student is being punished for the sins of someone else's parents. That is not right and it is not fair.

The Mexican government constantly lobbies our state governments to provide in-state tuition for illegal aliens. Maybe it's time for Mexico to take an active role in the education of its own citizens by providing scholarships and financial assistance to those wanting to attend American colleges and universities legally. There is no reason to saddle our education budgets with these costs while Mexico gets a free ride.

WHAT TO DO ABOUT WORKERS

It is a myth that Americans won't do jobs that are hard, dirty, or dangerous. But when someone else is willing to do it for minimum wage or less, well...

As I said earlier, it's not that illegals will take jobs Americans won't, but that they'll take *wages* Americans won't, and there are many unscrupulous businesses that are more than willing to oblige them.

Time was when Americans could raise families and enjoy a middle-class life on the salaries of the kinds of jobs illegal aliens now routinely do for peanuts. In a letter to the *Arizona Republic*, a worker laments: "I came to Arizona in 1998 to learn a trade. Unfortunately, I could not support myself on the wages that were being paid.... It used to be that a tradesman made a solid middle-class living. Not anymore. If you want to get into a trade, get ready to share a one-bedroom apartment with eight other people, because that is the only way you can make any money."[15]

When I was growing up in North Carolina, a summer job like picking crops or house painting or working at a drive-in restaurant was
considered a rite of passage and an essential character-forming experience that prepared young people for the responsibilities of adult-
hood. Illegal immigrants now fill many of these jobs, leaving many
young Americans, especially minority Americans, out of work. Illegal
immigration is part of the reason the past few years have been some of
the worst ever for teenage summer employment.

Still, America does need skilled immigrant workers to ensure a
growing economy and the future solvency of programs like Social Security and Medicare. High-tech jobs are critical to our economic future,
and our colleges and universities aren't producing enough high-tech
talent to meet our needs. With more options for talented people in a
global economy, we will have to compete as much for brainpower and
skilled workers as we do for investment capital or sales of our products.

So I propose that we end the diversity lottery program (see Chapter Two), which is riddled with fraud, and end the visa category that
allows immigrants to bring in their adult brothers and sisters. These
changes would eliminate 55,000 and 65,000 immigration slots respectively. I would transfer those 120,000 slots to the employment-based
immigration category and add another 80,000 for good measure. Then
I would give Citizenship and Immigration Services the resources to
end the backlogs and speed the process of getting these people here.
This would provide American businesses with 200,000 new slots every
year to fill needed positions where no American can truly be found.
And we'd be admitting into the country people who really want to
become Americans.

WHAT TO DO ABOUT MEXICO

We've all heard the old proverb that if you give a man a fish, it will feed
him for a day, but if you teach a man to fish, he can feed himself for a
lifetime. Decades of economic mismanagement has made the fishing
in Mexico so lousy that its government is forced to encourage its people to head north to fish without a permit. As a result, over large parts
of the Mexican workforce there hangs a sign saying, "Gone fishing."

It is impossible not to feel sympathy for the Mexican people struggling to survive in a country where economic backwardness and corruption rule the day. But Mexico will never solve its problems as long as the United States remains its economic safety valve. It is time we gave Mexico some tough love.

Every year, the U.S. allows more than 210,000 Mexicans to enter the country legally. A conservative estimate puts the number of illegal Mexicans in the country at five million, which is equal to at least twenty-five years worth of legal Mexican immigration! We simply cannot let that kind of theft—and it is a form of theft—go unpunished.

To stem this flood, we need not only to close the border to illegal immigrants, we need to impose a three-year ban on legal immigration from Mexico (this would not include tourists) that can either be repealed or renewed as dictated by Congress. This will create a domestic constituency in Mexico demanding that the Mexican government cooperate with the United States on illegal immigration.

Moreover, we should repeal the preferences Mexico receives in many visa categories. Mexicans should not be rewarded with preference over people from Asia, Africa, or anywhere else. And we should discourage "dual citizenship," a notion anathema to our oath of citizenship, which requires the renunciation of allegiances to any other country. Dual citizenship is inconsistent with our ideal of what it means to be American.

Teddy Roosevelt rightly called dual citizenship a "self-evident absurdity." But the solution is not as easy as banning dual citizenship. If Mexico (or any country) wants to continue recognizing as one of its citizens a Mexican who has become an American citizen, there is nothing we can do to prevent it. In addition, the courts have ruled that we cannot force someone to formally renounce their previous citizenship. We can, however, make it a felony for an American to exercise the rights of citizenship of another country. We should therefore impose a $10,000 fine and a year in jail for voting in a foreign election, serving in a foreign government, running for elective office in a foreign state, or serving in a foreign army.

We should prohibit the matrícula consular card from being accepted as a legitimate form of identification. These cards, which have made it easy for illegals to open bank accounts and get driver's licenses, are an integral part of the Mexican government's efforts to do an end run around our immigration laws and assist their citizens in settling here illegally. It is intolerable that while the FBI warns that terrorists could use the cards, the Treasury Department has decided to allow American banks to accept them. That decision must be overturned. The banks will squeal. Let them.

Finally, we should encourage the Mexicans to get their economic house in order so that this country can finally achieve the incredible economic potential that remains untapped. As author Luis Alberto Urrea put it: "Raise the standards in Mexico, and these good people will go home."[16]

WHAT CAN YOU DO?

The late African American journalist Tony Brown once declared, "The problem with depending on government is that you cannot depend on it."[17] If there is one thing we've learned, it is that when it comes to illegal immigration, we can't depend on the government to solve the problem. Americans tried that in 1986—and what happened? The politicians made the problem worse with an amnesty plan that triggered an unrelenting illegal invasion of our country. There has been nothing like it in our history.

America has a choice. We can either take control of our borders and our immigration policy, or we can leave those decisions to Mexican president Vicente Fox, drug smugglers, and terrorists.

In an appearance on Don Imus's radio program, Kinky Friedman, the Texas troubadour, author, raconteur, and gubernatorial candidate, described his proposal to eliminate illegal immigration, called the "Five Generals Plan."

Friedman proposed dividing Texas's border with Mexico into five sectors and choosing a Mexican general to be in charge of each one on the Mexican side. Their job would be to stop illegals from crossing the border in their sector. At the start of the program, one million dollars would be deposited into a bank account for each general. For every illegal alien caught coming across the border in a general's sector, $5,000 or so would be removed from that general's account. At the end of the year, the generals would get to keep whatever was left.

While I am not ready to introduce this plan in Congress, it does show a greater understanding of the illegal immigration problem and how to solve it than all the politicians and think tanks in Washington combined. It recognizes that as things stand now there is no incentive anywhere to stop illegal immigration, and that without some incentive, we might as well declare surrender and open the borders. That's where the American people come in.

The people need to provide the incentive by turning up the political heat. President Lyndon Johnson used to challenge Americans: "This is your country and we need to know what you want to do about it." I issue that same challenge.

Beginning here and now, let us resolve to do all we can to educate and mobilize the silent majority of Americans who agree that the status quo is not only intolerable, but dangerous to our nation.

So what can you do?

Americans can start by using the most potent tool in the arsenal of democracy—the vote. Let Congress and the White House feel the heat, the frustration, and yes, the anger of the American people.

Visit the websites of groups like the Center for Immigration Studies (www.cis.org), Numbers USA (www.numbersusa.com), Americans for Legal Immigration (www.alipac.us), and the Federation for American Immigration Reform (www.fairus.org). Contact the Minuteman Civil Defense Corps and the Minuteman Project (www.minutemanhq.com) to see how you can get involved. Another great website is Michelle Malkin's "The Immigration Blog." Share this book with your friends and neighbors so they can see exactly what is at stake and what we are up against. Call your local talk radio and write letters to your newspaper.

Make no mistake: we are already at a disadvantage. The special interests are organized and ready to go with a guest worker/amnesty plan that rewards illegal behavior and invites more illegal immigration.

Their "solution" is not about what is best for America, but what is best for them.

To counter them, I have drafted legislation in Congress, the "Enforcement First Immigration Reform Act," that incorporates many of the recommendations made in this chapter. No guest-worker plan, no amnesty, no reward for illegal behavior. It toughens our immigration laws and then provides the resources necessary to enforce them. Please visit my website for more information: http://hayworth.house.gov/.

Republican political strategist and pro-amnesty advocate Grover Norquist has said that on the politics of illegal immigration "intensity trumps preference."[18] In other words, Congress and the president will pay attention to the special interests looking to accommodate illegal immigration while ignoring the majority of the American people who want it stopped. I have traveled all around this great country of ours and on this issue I know the intensity for "enforcement first" is there. It is time for Americans to show it. Nature abhors a vacuum. Let's not leave the playing field to the special interests, or we will all wake up one day to a country in which *E pluribus unum* is nothing but a quaint expression from another time.

None of what I have suggested will be easy. Worthwhile causes rarely are. But I believe that if we can reclaim our borders and reinstill a respect for the rule of law, we will have pulled America back from the brink.

At a town hall meeting in my district in the wake of September 11, I discussed this very issue with a group of constituents. Arizona is on the front line of the illegal alien invasion, and every attendee was fed up with the government's dereliction and concerned about terrorists exploiting the chaos on our borders. I asked them how much they were willing to sacrifice to win the War on Terror, protect the homeland, and secure our borders. The reply from one constituent summed up the attitude of all of them: "Whatever it takes, congressman, whatever it takes."

To secure America's future, we must secure America's borders.

This is our call to action. Let's get the job done—whatever it takes.

ACKNOWLEDGMENTS

L IKE SUCCESS, A BOOK HAS MANY FATHERS. First among those who aided in this creative process was my chief of staff and co-author, Joe Eule. Joe kept me focused on the task at hand and helped me find the right words to convey just what's at stake in this debate. Two other valuable members of my staff, press secretary Larry VanHoose and legislative assistant Todd Sommers, also played important roles. Larry offered his critical eye and sound suggestions as he reviewed several rough drafts, while Todd chased down the facts and helped assemble the data that not only bolstered the arguments made in this book, but which also led to the introduction of H.R. 3938, the Enforcement First Immigration Reform Act. Erik Rasmussen, who handles health care and retirement issues in my office, also helped by untangling the effect of illegal immigration on Social Security.

Lee Habeeb, producer of the *Laura Ingraham Show*, proved that he possesses a discriminating eye for the printed word as well as a discerning ear for the sound bites he puts on the radio. His suggestions were most helpful. Harry Crocker and Paula Decker of Regnery Publishing likewise offered ideas, observations, encouragement...and first-rate editing. All those mentioned above helped me do whatever it took for *Whatever It Takes*.

NOTES

Chapter One
OVERRUN

1. Donald L. Barlett and James B. Steele, "Who Left the Door Open?" *Time*, September 20, 2004.
2. "Connecticut Town Struggles with Illegal Immigrants," FOX News, April 28, 2005. See http://www.foxnews.com/story/0,2933,154957,00.html.
3. Testimony of Michael Chertoff, secretary, Department of Homeland Security, before the Senate Judiciary Committee, October 18, 2005.
4. Jerry Kammer, "Loophole to America," Copley News Service, June 4, 2005.
5. Jeffrey Passel, "Unauthorized Migrants: Numbers and Characteristics," Pew Hispanic Center, June 14, 2005.
6. Robert Justich and Betty Ng, "The Underground Labor Force Is Rising to the Surface," Bear Stearns Asset Management, January 3, 2005.
7. Testimony by Nancy Kingsbury, managing director, Applied Research and Methods, Government Accountability Office, "Overstay Tracking Is a Key Component of a Layered Defense," October 16, 2003. See http://www.gao.gov/new.items/d04170t.pdf. Ms. Kingsbury testified before the House Subcommittee on Immigration, Border

Security, and Claims that: "Significant numbers of foreign visitors overstay their authorized periods of admission. The Department of Homeland Security estimates the resident overstay population at 2.3 million as of January 2000. Because the starting point for this estimate is the 2000 census, it does not cover short-term overstays who have not established residence here. It also omits an unknown number of potential long-term overstays from Mexico and Canada. Because of unresolved weaknesses in DHS's current system for tracking arrivals and departures (e.g., noncollection of some departure forms and inability to match other departure forms to arrivals), there is no accurate list of overstays."

8. CIA director Porter Goss, testimony before the Senate Select Committee on Intelligence, February 16, 2005.

9. Admiral James Loy, deputy secretary, Department of Homeland Security, testimony before the Senate Select Committee on Intelligence, February 16, 2005.

10. Susan Carroll, "Syrians caught; in U.S. illegally," *Arizona Republic*, March 18, 2005.

11. Robert Anglen, "Mesa man accused of smuggling Iranians," *Arizona Republic*, June 1, 2005.

12. Adam Zagorin, Timothy J. Burger, and Brian Bennett, "Zarqawi Planning U.S. Hit?" *Time*, March 21, 2005.

13. Kimberly Edds, "U.S. Calls Entry Point in San Diego a Possible Security Risk," *Washington Post*, March 10, 2005.

14. Honorable Chris Cox, chairman, Select Committee on Homeland Security, "In 2004, border patrol agents arrested over 650 suspected terrorists," press release, February 9, 2005.

15. Onell R. Soto and Leslie Berestein, "Border agent said to also be smuggler," *San Diego Union-Tribune*, August 5, 2005.

16. Admiral James Loy, deputy secretary, Department of Homeland Security, testimony before the Senate Select Committee on Intelligence, February 16, 2005.

17. Stewart Bell, *Cold Terror: How Canada Nurtures and Exports Terror Around the World* (New York: John Wiley & Sons), 2005.

18. Stewart Bell, "What do you do when a jihadi comes home?" *National Post*, March 4, 2005.

19. Beth Duff-Brown and Pauline Arrillaga, "U.S.–Canada Border Leaves Many Jittery," Associated Press, July 4, 2005.

20. *9-11 Commission Report*, August 2004, 401.

21. Janice Kephart, "Immigration and Terror: Moving Beyond the 9/11 Staff Report on Terrorist Travel," Center for Immigration Studies, September 2005.

22. "Review of the Immigration and Customs Enforcement's Compliance Enforcement Unit," Office of Inspector General, Department of Homeland Security, September 2005.

23. "Immigrants and Terrorists," *Wall Street Journal*, March 18, 2002.

24. Lee Morgan, quoted by Tamar Jacoby, "Law and Borders: The conservative case for Bush's immigration plan," *Weekly Standard*, February 28, 2005.

25. Federal Document Clearing House, Congressional Testimony, February 13, 2004. Capitol Hill hearing testimony, House International Relations, "Preventing Terrorism from Entering the United States," William D. West, retired supervisory special agent, U.S. Immigration and Naturalization Service.

26. Leo W. Banks, "Minutemen Are People, Too," *Wall Street Journal*, May 19, 2005.

27. Federal Document Clearing House, Congressional Testimony, February 16, 2005. Capitol Hill hearing testimony, Senate Indian Affairs, fiscal 2006 budget: Indian Affairs, Tex Hall, president, National Congress of American Indians.

28. Hernan Rozemberg, "Making a stand on the border; Minuteman Project aims to police migrants in Arizona, but leaders reject vigilante label," *San Antonio Express-News*, February 21, 2005.

29. Claudine LoMonaco, "Burglars make off with congressman's clothes," *Tucson Citizen*, August 4, 2005.

30. Karen Schaler, "Border crossings hinder training at Arizona bases," *Boston Globe*, April 7, 2005.

31. Bill Richardson, "Aliens over armed forces," *East Valley Tribune*, May 13, 2005.

32. Barlett and Steele, "Who Left the Door Open?" *Time*, September 20, 2004. To its credit, Tyson Foods has worked hard to reform its suspect hiring practices.

33. Charles V. Zehren, "Tough times for honest employers," *Newsday*, June 5, 2005.
34. Senator Edward Kennedy, speech delivered at the Center for Humanities, City University of New York, "Creating a Genuine Opportunity Society," March 1, 2004.
35. Statement by Senator Edward Kennedy, Senate floor, May 12, 2005.
36. Dr. George Borjas, "Increasing the Supply of Labor through Immigration: Measuring the impact on native-born workers," Center for Immigration Studies, May 2004.
37. "Immigrants and Terrorists," *Wall Street Journal*, March 18, 2002.
38. Bill Searle, "Guest worker proposal doesn't mock U.S. principles," *Arizona Republic*, February 17, 2005.
39. Global Views 2004: American Public Opinion and Foreign Policy, Chicago Council on Foreign Relations, 2004. See http://www.ccfr.org/globalviews2004/sub/pdf/Global_Views_2004_US.pdf.
40. Justich and Ng, "The Underground Labor Force Is Rising to the Surface."
41. Brian Gatton, "Action needed to stem illegal-immigration tide," *Arizona Republic*, August 28, 2005.
42. "Flow of Undocumented Mexicans into U.S. Expected to Continue at Same Pace as Recent Years: Mexico to Press for Immigration Accord," *SourceMex Economic News & Analysis on Mexico*, January 12, 2005.
43. Jack Martin, "Breaking the Piggy Bank: How Illegal Immigration Is Sending Schools into the Red," Federation for American Immigration Reform, June 2005.
44. Maria Newman, "School District Blocks 5 Children of Illegal Immigrants from Classes," *New York Times*, September 21, 2002.
45. Susan Carroll, "State Slow to Investigate Border-Hopping Students," *Arizona Republic*, April 30, 2005.
46. Ibid.
47. Victor Davis Hanson, "Illiberal Aspects of Illegal Immigration," Tribune Media Services, June 13, 2005.
48. "L.A. Emergency Rooms Full of Illegal Immigrants," FOX News, March 18, 2005.
49. Barlett and Steele, "Who Left the Door Open?"

50. Joyce Howard Price, "Disease, unwanted import," *Washington Times*, February 13, 2005.

51. Madeleine Cosman, Ph.D., Esq., "Illegal Aliens and American Medicine," *Journal of American Physicians and Surgeons*, Volume 10, Number 1, Spring 2005.

52. "Illegal Immigration and Public Health," Federation for American Immigration Reform. See http://www.fairus.org/site/ PageServer?pagename=iic_immigrationissuecenters64bf.

53. Barlett and Steele, "Who Left the Door Open?"

54. Representative Sheila Jackson-Lee, speech on floor of U.S. House of Representatives, September 9, 2004.

55. Sarita A. Mohanty, Steffie Woolhandler, David U. Himmelstein, Susmita Pati, Olveen Carrasquillo, and David H. Bor, "Health Care Expenditures of Immigrants in the United States: A Nationally Representative Analysis," *American Journal of Public Health*, August 2005.

56. Price, "Disease, unwanted import."

57. Jane Daugherty, "Perilous Infectious Diseases up in County," *Palm Beach Post*, July 24, 2005.

58. Cosman, "Illegal Aliens and American Medicine."

Chapter Two
CRIME AND ILLEGAL IMMIGRATION

1. Alfredo Corchado, "Mexican Zetas extending violence into U.S., officials say," *Dallas Morning News*, February 20, 2005.

2. "Never Acceptable," *Arizona Republic*, May 26, 2005.

3. Statement by Senator John McCain, Senate floor, May 12, 2005.

4. Billy House and Susan Carroll, "Migration reform not anticipated during '05," *Arizona Republic*, July 15, 2005.

5. "Alien Abduction," *Investor's Business Daily*, May 25, 2005.

6. "Information on Criminal Aliens Incarcerated in Federal and State Prisons and Local Jails," Government Accountability Office, March 29, 2005.

7. "Information on Certain Illegal Aliens Arrested in the United States," Government Accountability Office, April 2005.

8. Ibid.
9. Heather Mac Donald, "The Illegal Alien Crime Wave," *City Journal*, Winter 2004.
10. Testimony of Kris W. Kobach before the Immigration, Border Security, and Claims Subcommittee of the House Judiciary Committee, June 28, 2005.
11. Arian Campos-Flores, "The Most Dangerous Gang in America," *Newsweek*, March 28, 2005.
12. U.S. Department of Justice, FBI, Crime in the United States, 2002 Uniform Crime Reports.
13. "Desert wildlife researchers face border perils," KVOA Eyewitness News 4, Tucson, August 8, 2005.
14. Statement of John Feinblatt, criminal justice coordinator, City of New York, before the Subcommittee on Immigration, Border Security, and Claims, House Committee on the Judiciary, February 27, 2003.
15. Carol Platt Liebau, "Equal Treatment for L.A.'s Criminals," *Los Angeles Times*, May 15, 2005.
16. Heather Mac Donald, "Illegal Immigrants to Get More Constitutional Rights Than Citizens," Immigration Blog, March 31, 2005. See http://michellemalkin.com/immigration/2005/03/31/10:06.am.
17. ACLU Press release, "ACLU Says LAPD Unit Used Deportation Threat to Retaliate Against Immigrant Whistle Blower," January 25, 2000.
18. Letter to Honorable Charlie Norwood, February 17, 2004.
19. Michael Janofsky, "Phoenix Counts Its Many Challenges," *New York Times*, April 11, 2001.
20. Anna Gorman, "Illegal Immigrants Who Aided Police Sue for Federal Visas," *Los Angeles Times*, October 19, 2005.
21. Jonathan Cohn, deputy assistant attorney general for the civil division, U.S. Department of Justice, Testimony before the Senate Committee on the Judiciary Subcommittee on Immigration, Border Security, and Citizenship, April 14, 2005.
22. Mac Donald, "The Illegal Alien Crime Wave."
23. The Immigration and Naturalization Service's Removal of Aliens Issued Final Orders, Report Number I-2003-004, February 2003, i.

24. Anna Gorman, "Suspects Chafing in Ankle Monitors," *Los Angeles Times*, June 21, 2005.

25. Ibid.

26. Bill Richardson, "Let feds end laxity on enforcement," *East Valley Tribune*, October 14, 2005.

27. H. G. Reza, "Minor Offenders in Orange County Taken to Border Patrol," *Los Angeles Times*, February 12, 2001.

28. John Futty, "Fire-Rescue Goals Issued: Panel recommends changes after blaze that killed 10," *Columbus Dispatch*, December 22, 2004.

29. Ibid.

30. Ibid.

31. "Mexico is trying an end run around Congress," *Chicago Sun-Times*, February 15, 2003.

32. Brian DeBose, "Police won't ask aliens of status, Ramsey assures city's Hispanics," *Washington Times*, July 29, 2003.

33. E-mail sent on October 30, 2002, by Robin F. Baker, assistant regional director for the INS, to about fifty other INS employees. Quoted by Michelle Malkin in "Who'll protect the whistleblowers?" TownHall.com, November 13, 2002. See http://www.townhall.com/columnists/michellemalkin/mm20021113.shtml.

34. "9/11 and Terrorist Travel; Staff Report of the National Commissions on Terrorist Attacks Upon the United States," August 21, 2004, 160.

35. Editor's note to op-ed by Congressman J. D. Hayworth, "Attack on alien removal act unfair," *Arizona Republic*, November 10, 2003.

36. Michael Powell, "New Tack Against Illegal Immigrants: Trespassing Charges," *Washington Post*, June 10, 2005.

37. Ibid.

38. Melissa Tyrrell, "Fearing crackdown, Elsmere's Latinos keep low profile; Councilman's proposal would fine residents who are undocumented," *New Journal*, April 16, 2005.

39. Ibid.

40. Dan Walters, "New issues rekindle California's angst over illegal immigration," *Sacramento Bee*, July 20, 2005.

41. Stewart Bell, *Cold Terror: How Canada Nurtures and Exports Terror Around the World* (New York: John Wiley & Sons, 2005).

42. The Immigration and Naturalization Service's Removal of Aliens Issued Final Orders, Report Number I-2003-004, February 2003, v.

Chapter Three
ASSIMILATION: OUT OF MANY... ?

1. Samuel P. Huntington, *Who Are We: The Challenges to America's National Identity* (New York: Simon & Schuster, 2004).
2. Alistair Cooke, *The Patient Has the Floor* (Franklin Center, PA: Franklin Institute, 1986).
3. Huntington.
4. Robert J. Samuelson, "Candor on Immigration," *Washington Post*, June 8, 2005.
5. Mark Steyn, "Bicultural Europe is doomed," *Telegraph*, November 15, 2005.
6. Charles Krauthammer, "Assimilation Nation," *Washington Post*, June 17, 2005.
7. Frank Rodriguez, Letter to the Editor, *Los Angeles Times*, February 21, 1998.
8. Grahame L. Jones, "This Is Much Worse Than Trash Talking," *Los Angeles Times*, February 16, 1998.
9. Paul von Zielbauer, "Hartford Bids a Bilingual Goodbye to a White-Collar Past," *New York Times*, May 5, 2003.
10. Juan Hernandez, *Nightline*, ABC News, June 7, 2001.
11. Huntington.
12. Phyllis Schlafly, "Is it assimilation or invasion?" *Washington Times*, November 24, 2001.
13. Heather Mac Donald, "Mexico's Undiplomatic Diplomats," *City Journal*, Autumn 2005.
14. "Mexican Immigration and Its Potential Impact on the Political Future of the United States," Yeh Ling-Ling, *Journal of Social, Political and Economic Studies*, Volume 29, Number 4, Winter 2004.
15. Ernest Cienfuegos, "Mexico requests that apartment fire that killed 10 immigrants be investigated as a possible racial attack," *La*

Voz de Aztlán, September 20, 2004. See http://www.aztlan.net/ mexico_investigate_racial_attack.htm.

16. Mark Steyn, "A victory for multiculti over common sense," *Daily Telegraph*, July 19, 2005.

17. Paul Belien, "Show them who is boss in Brussels," *Brussels Journal*, November 6, 2005.

18. Tony Blankley, *The West's Last Chance* (Washington, D.C.: Regnery, 2005), 75.

19. Huntington.

20. Panel discussion transcript, 2005 Eugene Katz Award for Excellence in the Coverage of Immigration, National Press Club, Washington, D.C., June 3, 2005. See http://www.cis.org/articles/Katz/ katzpanel2005.html.

21. Yvonne Wingett, "Latinos, migrants face clash of cultures," *Arizona Republic*, October 7, 2005.

Chapter Four

LANGUAGE, POLITICAL CORRECTNESS, AND ILLEGAL IMMIGRATION

1. Richard DeUriarte, "Communities Adjoin but Are Worlds Apart," *Phoenix Gazette*, March 14, 1993.

2. Jane Thynne, "Into the Dark: The Reporter the Men of Violence Talk to," *Independent on Sunday* (London), July 24, 2005.

3. Daniel Gonzalez, "Undocumented immigrant family embraces middle-class America," *Arizona Republic*, October 17, 2005.

4. Heather Mac Donald, "The Illegal Alien Crime Wave," *City Journal*, Winter 2004.

5. Eunice Moscoso, "Immigration Proponents Choose Words Carefully," Cox News Service, August 15, 2001.

6. Yvonne Wingett, "Fiery Voice for Immigrants," *Arizona Republic*, July 10, 2005.

7. *Hannity & Colmes*, FOX News Network, March 26, 2002.

8. Ruben Navarrette Jr., "The problem we can fix," *San Diego Union-Tribune*, March 23, 2005.

9. James C. McKinley Jr., "At Mexican Border, Tunnels, Vile River, Rusty Fence," *New York Times*, March 23, 2005.

10. Press Release, "Catholic Bishops Launch Immigration Reform Campaign," United States Conference of Catholic Bishops, May 10, 2005.

11. Congressional Record, June 18, 2004.

12. Manuel Gutiérrez Fierro, "Vidas Públicas," *La Voz*, azcentral.com, August 3, 2005. See http://calcutta.azcentral.com/lavoz/editorial/articles/0803vidaspublicas-CR.html.

13. Amy Lorentzen, "King hosts illegal immigration forum," Associated Press, August 22, 2005.

14. Salvador Reza, "What is it about Mexicans? We don't forget where we came from," *Arizona Republic*, January 31, 2005.

15. Debra J. Saunders, "Let my illegal nanny drive my SUV," *San Francisco Chronicle*, February 3, 2005.

16. "Stonewall Simpson," *Wall Street Journal*, October 12, 1990.

17. See http://www.mta.net/about_us/metroart/ma_mlnkbjb.htm.

18. David Pierson and Wendy Lee, "A Monumental War of Words," *Los Angeles Times*, June 25, 2005.

19. "Minutemess Patrol," *Arizona Republic*, March 9, 2005.

20. Jerry Seper, "ACLU to keep tabs on protest," *Washington Times*, March 21, 2005.

21. "Concerns over possible violence grow among Arizona-Sonora border's residents," *El Universal* (Mexico), April 1, 2005.

22. Arthur H. Rothstein, "April's volunteer border watch project focus of controversy," Associated Press, March 26, 2005.

23. Chris Richard, "Immigration group protests border watch," *Press-Enterprise* (Riverside, CA), March 19, 2005.

24. Chris Ziegler, "Fear and Loathing on the Camping Trail," *OC Weekly*, April 22, 2005.

25. "Mexico-US: Governors send vitriolic letter to Arnie," *Latin American Weekly Report*, May 31, 2005.

26. Sarah Vowell, "Lock and Load," *New York Times*, July 23, 2005.

27. "Bush Meets with Mexican President Fox, Canadian Prime Minister Martin," *US Fed News* (Waco, TX), March 23, 2005.

28. Arthur Rothstein, "Border watch volunteers wrap up month along Arizona border," Associated Press, April 30, 2005.

29. "More Than a Minute," *Arizona Republic*, May 8, 2005.

30. Press release, "GOP Says Hispanics Are 'Enemies of the State,' Democrats Fight Back," Democratic Congressional Campaign Committee, February 14, 2002.

31. For corroboration, see "The DCCC's Dirty Tricks," *Weekly Standard*, March 4, 2002.

32. Lloyd Grove, "Reliable Source," *Washington Post*, February 15, 2002.

Chapter Five
MEXICO: FRIEND OR FOE?

1. Julie Weise, "Border Czar Ruffo: Economics Is Key to Solving Region's Woes," *The News*, March 8, 2001.

2. Testimony of Steven McGraw, assistant director, Office of Intelligence, FBI, before the Subcommittee on Immigration, Border Security, and Claims of the House Committee on the Judiciary, June 19, 2003.

3. Traci Carl, "Mexico says it will protest new U.S. immigration laws," Associated Press, May 12, 2005.

4. Edward Alden and John Authers, "Mexico furious at tough US law on migrants," *Financial Times* (London), May 14, 2005.

5. Ibid.

6. Luis Alberto Urrea, "America's bounty for Mexico," *Arizona Republic*, June 12, 2005.

7. Laurence Iliff, "Mexico cracking down on migrants on southern border," *Dallas Morning News*, August 18, 2001.

8. Chris Hawley, "Yucatan Helping Migrants Go North; Guide, DVD Show Mexicans How to Cross Border, Send Cash Home," *Arizona Republic*, February 18, 2005.

9. Chris Hawley, "In the highlands of Oaxaca, a town struggles to survive," *Arizona Republic*, May 15, 2005.

10. Francisco J. Alejo, consul general of Mexico, "The facts on Mexico's guide for immigrants," *Austin American-Statesman* (Texas), January 21, 2005. Geronimo Gutierrez, Mexican undersecretary for North America, made an identical remark in an op-ed in the *Arizona Republic* ("Immigration Guide Stresses Safety") on January 9, 2005.

11. "Maize and Biodiversity: The Effects of Transgenic Maize in Mexico," Commission for Environmental Cooperation of North America, November 8, 2004.

12. Marc Kaufman, "U.S. Genetically Modified Corn Is Assailed; NAFTA Report Calls Grain a Threat to Mexico," *Washington Post*, November 10, 2004.

13. "Maize and Biodiversity; The Effects of Transgenic Maize in Mexico."

14. Statement of Mark K. Reed before the Subcommittee on Immigration, Border Security, and Citizenship and the Subcommittee on Terrorism, Technology, and Homeland Security, May 17, 2005.

15. Mark Steyn, "Bush's Strategy, Assessed," *National Review*, September 26, 2005.

16. David Luna, "Over a Barrel," *Wall Street Journal*, June 15, 2005.

17. Marc A. Miles, Edwin J. Feulner, and Mary Anastasia O'Grady, "2005 Index of Economic Freedom," Heritage Foundation, 2005.

18. Chris Hawley, "Mexico defends its policy on oil after U.S. comment," *Arizona Republic*, May 22, 2005.

19. Luis Alberto Urrea, "America's bounty for Mexico," *Arizona Republic*, June 12, 2005.

20. Glynn Custred, "North American Borders: Why They Matter," Center for Immigration Studies, April 2003.

21. Sonia Nazario, "Enrique's Journey/Chapter Three: Defeated Seven Times, a Boy Again Faces 'the Beast,'" *Los Angeles Times*, October 2, 2002.

22. Chris Hawley, "Mexico Has a Problem with Migrants Too," *Arizona Republic*, July 28, 2005.

23. George W. Grayson, "Mexico's Forgotten Southern Border," Center for Immigration Studies, July 2002.

24. Velia Jaramillo, "Mexico's 'Southern Plan': The Facts," *Proceso* (Mexico), June 26, 2001.

25. Hawley, "Mexico Has a Problem with Migrants Too."

26. George W. Grayson, "Mexico's Forgotten Southern Border," Center for Immigration Studies, July 2002.

27. Ibid.

28. James C. McKinley, Jr., "At Mexican Border, Tunnels, Vile River, Rusty Fence," *New York Times*, March 23, 2005.

29. Roberto Suro, Pew Hispanic Center, "Attitudes toward Immigrants and Immigration Policy: Surveys among Latinos in the U.S. and in Mexico," Pew Hispanic Center, August 16, 2005.

30. "Is Mexico still a nation?" *Christian Science Monitor*, August 24, 2005.

Chapter Six
IS AMERICA COMPLICIT IN ILLEGAL IMMIGRATION?

1. Dan Eggen, "Ridge Revives Debate on Immigrant Status," *Washington Post*, December 11, 2003.

2. Donald L. Barlett and James B. Steele, "Who Left the Door Open?" *Time*, September 20, 2004.

3. Brian Grow, "Embracing Illegals," *BusinessWeek*, July 18, 2005.

4. Richard Gonzalez, "Businesses Target Illegal Immigrants," All Things Considered, NPR, July 18, 2005.

5. Ibid.

6. Grow, "Embracing Illegals."

7. Jonathan Higuera and Daniel Gonazlez, "Boon or bane, immigrants," *Arizona Republic*, October 17, 2005.

8. "BofA launches free remittance service to Mexico," *Charlotte Business Journal*, September 28, 2005.

9. Daniel Gonzalez, "Undocumented immigrant family embraces middle-class America," *Arizona Republic*, October 17, 2005.

10. Grow, "Embracing Illegals."

11. "Hope Over Experience," *National Review*, May 17, 2005.

12. Peter Wallsten and Nicole Gaouette, "Immigration Rising on Bush's To-Do List," *Los Angeles Times*, July 24, 2005

13. Public Papers of the Presidents, 22 Weekly Comp. Doc. 1534, Immigration Reform and Control Act of 1986, Statement on Signing S. 1200 into Law, November 6, 1986.

14. Representative Robert Garcia, Letter to the Editor, *New York Times*, November 6, 1984.

15. Congressional Record: Senate, October 16, 1986, 32377.

16. Congressional Record: House, October 15, 1986, 31635.

17. Lawrence H. Fuchs, "Good Immigrant Bill," *New York Times*, October 9, 1984.

18. Congressional Record: Senate, October 17, 1986, 33213.
19. James Rowley, "Pilot Program Announced to Help Verify Social Security Numbers," Associated Press, December 18, 1986.
20. Congressional Record: Senate, October 17, 1986, 33208.
21. Charles E. Schumer, "Back to Immigration," *New York Times*, May 21, 1985.
22. Larry Rother, "Mexicans Crowd a Last Opening to U.S.," *New York Times*, June 20, 1988.
23. Lucy Conger, "Mexican scholars disdain U.S. immigration legislation," *Phoenix Gazette*, November 1, 1986.
24. Michael Powell, "An Exodus Grows in Brooklyn," *Washington Post*, May 29, 2003.

Chapter Seven
THE LEFT AND RIGHT ARE WRONG

1. Interview on National Public Radio's Morning Edition, March 2, 2004.
2. David Frum, "GOP, You Are Warned," *National Review*, December 31, 2004.
3. "In Praise of Huddled Masses," *Wall Street Journal*, July 3, 1984.
4. "Thinking Things Over: Open Nafta Borders? Why Not?" *Wall Street Journal*, July 2, 2001.
5. "Immigrant Realities," *Wall Street Journal*, January 9, 2004.
6. "Our Border Brigades," *Wall Street Journal*, January 27, 2004.
7. Jason Riley, "GOP Nativists Tarnish Reagan's 'Shining City,'" *Wall Street Journal*, March 15, 2004.
8. "Utah Lawmaker Pushes for Illegal Alien Amnesty," *FOX News*, April 1, 2004. See http://www.foxnews.com/story/ 0,2933,115803,00.html.
9. Ralph de Unamuno, "The Facts Behind the Myths: FOX News, the GOP, and MEChA." See http://www.azteca.net/aztec/mecha/ MechaFact-Myths.html.
10. "Tighter US immigration policy expected following attacks," Agence France Presse, September 13, 2001.
11. *Lou Dobbs Tonight*, CNN, June 9, 2005.

12. Statement by Senator Edward Kennedy, Senate floor, May 12, 2005.

13. Ibid.

14. Mike Lentino, Letter to the Editor, *Arizona Republic*, May 19, 2005.

15. Susan Carroll, "Who will work the fields?" *Arizona Republic*, November 3, 2005.

16. Philip Martin, "How We Eat: 2002, Obesity," Rural Migration News.

17. Mark Krikorian, "More Guest Workers? Not What We Should Pick," *Washington Post*, February 25, 2001.

18. Dean E. Murphy, "Imagining Life Without Illegal Immigrants," *New York Times*, January 11, 2004.

19. Matthew Dowd, "The Mexican Evolution," *New York Times*, August 1, 2005.

20. Joel Millman, "A New Future for Mexico's Work Force: Hot Job Market Eases Pressure to Go to U.S.," *Wall Street Journal*, April 14, 2000.

21. Mark Krikorian, "Ay Caramba!" National Review Online, August 3, 2005.

Chapter Eight
IS ILLEGAL IMMIGRATION
THE ANSWER TO SOCIAL SECURITY?

1. Luis Alberto Urrea, "America's bounty for Mexico," *Arizona Republic*, June 12, 2005.

2. "The Old and the New: Immigrants play a key role in Social Security," *Wall Street Journal*, March 10, 2005.

3. Eduardo Porter, "Illegal Immigrants Are Bolstering Social Security with Billions," *New York Times*, April 5, 2005.

4. Urrea, "America's bounty for Mexico."

5. Stuart Anderson, "The Contribution of Legal Immigration to the Social Security System," National Foundation for American Policy, March 2005.

6. Jon Sarche, "Authorities Disrupt Counterfeit ID Ring," Associated Press, July 20, 2005.

7. Audit Report, Office of the Inspector General, Social Security Administration, "Employers with the Most Suspended Wage Items in the 5-Year Period 1997 through 2001," October 2004.

8. "Better Coordination among Federal Agencies Could Reduce Unidentified Earnings Reports," Government Accountability Office, February 2005.

9. Daniel Gonzalez, "Undocumented immigrant family embraces middle-class America," *Arizona Republic*, October 17, 2005.

10. Karen E. Crummy, "Workers' status is complex business," *Denver Post*, July 18, 2005.

11. Ibid.

12. Abstract, "Tax Administration: IRS Needs to Consider Options for Revising Regulations to Increase the Accuracy of Social Security Numbers on Wage Statements," GAO-04-712, Government Accountability Office, August 31, 2004.

13. Statement of the Honorable James B. Lockhart III, deputy commissioner, Social Security Administration, Testimony before the Subcommittee on Oversight of the House Committee on Ways and Means, March 10, 2004.

14. Daniel Gonzalez, "Few Firms Use Migrant ID Service," *Arizona Republic*, June 11, 2005.

15. "Better Coordination among Federal Agencies Could Reduce Unidentified Earnings Reports."

16. Statement of the Honorable Mark W. Everson, commissioner, Internal Revenue Service, Testimony before the Subcommittee on Oversight of the House Committee on Ways and Means, March 10, 2004.

17. Porter, "Illegal Immigrants Are Bolstering Social Security with Billions."

18. George L. Willis, Esq., Testimony Submitted to the Subcommittee on Oversight of the House Committee on Ways and Means, March 24, 2004.

19. Cindy Gonzalez, "Two women, one ID and plenty of problems," *Omaha-World Herald*, November 22, 2002.

20. Statement of Barbara D. Bovbjerg, director, Education, Workforce, and Income Security Issues, "Proposed Totalization Agreement with Mexico Presents Unique Challenges," GAO-03-1035T, Government Accountability Office, September 11, 2003.

21. Ibid.

22. David Nuschler and Alison Siskin, "Social Security Benefits for Noncitizens: Current Policy and Legislation," RL-32004, Congressional Research Service, May 11, 2005.

23. Eduardo Porter, "Social Security: Migrants Offer Numbers for Fee," *New York Times*, June 7, 2005.

24. Miriam Jordan, "Welcome Mat: Banks Open Doors to New Customers—Illegal Immigrants," *Wall Street Journal*, July 8, 2005.

25. Ibid.

Chapter Nine
GUEST WORKER = AMNESTY = SURRENDER

1. Testimony of Dr. Vernon Briggs, Professor of Industrial and Labor Relations, Cornell University, before the Subcommittee on Immigration and Border Security of the Judiciary Committee of the Senate, February 5, 2004.

2. Ibid.

3. Victor Davis Hanson, "Guest Workers by Any Other Name: 'Helots,'" *Investor's Business Daily*, August 12, 2005.

4. Hesburgh's six reasons for opposing a temporary-worker program were (1) it would be hard to set and enforce limits on a temporary-worker program; (2) once it was started, we'd never be able to end it; (3) certain sectors of the economy would become dependent on foreign labor; (4) certain jobs would be stigmatized as fit only for aliens; (5) it would establish an unprotected second class of aliens; (6) without strict enforcement, illegal aliens would continue to cross the border and the goal of cutting illegal immigration would fail.

5. Testimony of Dr. Vernon Briggs, February 5, 2004.

6. Statement by President Clinton on New Guest-Worker Program, White House Press Office, U.S. Newswire, June 23, 1995.

7. Tamar Jacoby, "Law and Borders: The conservative case for Bush's immigration plan," *Weekly Standard*, February 28, 2005.

8. "Borderline Republicans," *Wall Street Journal*, June 17, 2004. See also Jason Riley, "GOP Nativists Tarnish Reagan's 'Shining City,'" *Wall Street Journal*, March 15, 2004.

9. Ruben Navarette, "Looking Ahead at the Bush Immigration Plan," *San Diego Union-Tribune*, October 12, 2005.

10. "Sanity, Not Amnesty," *Arizona Republic*, May 13, 2005.

11. Statement by Senator Edward Kennedy, Senate floor, May 12, 2005.

12. "Hope Over Experience," *National Review*, May 17, 2005.

13. Ruben Navarette, "Latino Advancement Requires Realistic Thinking," *San Diego Union-Tribune*, October 23, 2005.

14. Kevin Rogers, "Find a Path for Legal Outside Labor," *Arizona Republic*, January 20, 2005.

15. Michelle Mittelstadt, "Legalization, amnesty or what?" *Dallas Morning News*, August 9, 2001.

16. C. T. Revere, "Hastert: Immigration reform at top of to-do list," *Tucson Citizen*, August 25, 2005.

17. Statement by Senator Edward Kennedy, Senate floor, May 12, 2005.

18. Congressional Record-Senate, October 16, 1986, 32410.

19. Ibid., 32377.

20. Todd J. Gillmann and Alfredo Corchado, "Fox presses U.S. to give legal status to migrants," *Dallas Morning News*, July 18, 2001.

21. Donald L. Barlett and James B. Steele, "Who Left the Door Open?" *Time*, September 20, 2004.

22. Luis Alberto Urrea, "America's bounty for Mexico," *Arizona Republic*, June 12, 2005.

23. Joel Millman, "Border-Jumping from Mexico Surges," *Wall Street Journal*, April 29, 2004.

24. "U.S. Border Patrol Survey Analysis," Judicial Watch, June 28, 2005.

25. Richard Chesnoff, "A war of the worlds," *New York Daily News*, November 7, 2005.

26. "Survey of Mexican Migrants," Pew Hispanic Center, March 2, 2005.

27. Susan Carroll, Pat Flannery, Yvonne Wingett, and Jon Kamman, "Bush: Secure border but amnesty is out," *Arizona Republic*, November 29, 2005.

28. Anthony DePalma, "15 Years on the Bottom Rung," *New York Times*, May 26, 2005.

29. Daniel Gonzalez, "Citizen by birth? Perhaps not," *Arizona Republic*, November 25, 2005.

30. "Border States Grapple with Alien Criminals," FOX News, March 17, 2005.

31. Sergio Bustos, "Panel warns against major guest-worker program," *USA Today*, April 28, 2004.

32. Dan Bilefsky, "Belgian Experiment: Make Prostitution Legal to Fight Its Ills," *Wall Street Journal*, May 26, 2005.

33. Ibid.

34. Ibid.

35. Ibid.

36. Giles Tremlett, "Spain grants amnesty for 700,000 migrants," *Guardian*, May 9, 2005.

37. Renee Montagne, "Analysis: Illegal immigrants in Spain offered amnesty by government," NPR Morning Edition, January 18, 2005.

38. Bilefsky, "Belgian Experiment: Make Prostitution Legal to Fight Its Ills."

39. "Realistic Reform," *Arizona Republic*, January 23, 2005.

40. Representative Jeff Flake, "Bush amnesty plan is tougher than critics' version," *Tucson Citizen*, February 23, 2005.

41. Tamar Jacoby, "Getting Beyond the 'A-Word,'" *Wall Street Journal*, June 20, 2005.

42. Mike McCloy and John Dougherty, "Immigration bill gains despite Arizona opposition," *Phoenix Gazette*, October 15, 1986.

43. Martha Reinke, "Businesses Say Immigration Law Won't Affect Arizona Labor Pool," *Greater Phoenix Business Journal*, November 3, 1986.

Chapter Ten

IS OPPOSING ILLEGAL IMMIGRATION A POLITICAL LOSER FOR REPUBLICANS?

1. Andrew Miga, "Bush warms to illegal workers, but Dems rip plan as politics," *Boston Herald*, January 8, 2004.

2. Ricardo Alonso-Zaldivar, "Catch-22 Seen in Immigration Plan," *Los Angeles Times*, January 9, 2004.

3. "Bush calls for changes on illegal workers," CNN.com, January 7, 2004.

4. Juliana Barbassa, "Mexican migrant workers oppose Bush immigration proposal," Associated Press, January 14, 2004.
5. Michelle Malkin, "Open Doors for Hezbollah," *National Review*, November 14, 2002.
6. Election results, CNN.com, posted February 10, 2005.
7. Lourdes Medrano and Enric Volante, "Prop. 200 had Hispanic Support," *Arizona Daily Star*, November 4, 2004.
8. "Foreign secretary says Mexico may ask international courts to block Proposition 200," Associated Press, January 26, 2005.
9. Ibid.
10. "Attitudes toward Immigrants and Immigration Policy," Pew Hispanic Center, August 16, 2005.
11. Ibid.
12. Ibid.
13. "2002 National Survey of Latinos," Pew Hispanic Center/Kaiser Family Foundation, December 2002.
14. Ibid.
15. Steven Saint, "His Own Man," Hispanic Magazine.com, March 2004. See http://www.hispaniconline.com/magazine/2004/march/Career/.
16. "Attitudes toward Immigrants and Immigration Policy."
17. Jaime Castillo, "Democrats are looking in the wrong place for their lost votes," *San Antonio Express-News*, August 6, 2005.
18. John Gambling Show, WABC Radio, New York, February 2003.
19. *Hardball*, MSNBC, August 17, 2005.
20. Debra Dominguez, "Gathering Promotes 'Workers' Rights," *Albuquerque Journal*, September 26, 2003.
21. Chris Hawley, "Mexico report: Ariz. 'xenophobia' hotbed," *Arizona Republic*, April 3, 2005.
22. Ibid.
23. Ibid.
24. Ibid.
25. Press release, "Americans Support Common-Sense Immigration Reform," American Immigration Lawyers Association, April 7, 2005.
26. Tamar Jacoby, "The GOP's Border War," *Los Angeles Times*, October 16, 2005.

27. "No turning tail," *Arizona Republic*, November 18, 2005.
28. "Primary Colors," *Wall Street Journal*, September 13, 2004.
29. Jean O. Pasco, "O.C. Race Shapes Up as a Duel," *Los Angeles Times*, October 6, 2005.

Chapter Eleven
WHAT TO DO ABOUT ILLEGAL IMMIGRATION

1. Bill Stall and Tracy Wilkinson, "Bono Jumps into GOP Candidates Debate Politics: He says Senate primary opponents Campbell and Herschensohn are out of touch with mainstream Republicans," *Los Angles Times*, February 1, 1992.
2. Bill Richardson, "Let feds end laxity on enforcement," *East Valley Tribune*, October 14, 2005.
3. Leon Daniel, "America's borders are out of control: Congress tackles illegal immigration," United Press International, November 27, 1983.
4. Michelle Volkmann, "Range Sensors Saving Lives," *Yuma Sun*, March 12, 2005.
5. "Bush and Katrina," *Wall Street Journal*, September 6, 2005.
6. Scott Goldstein, "187 Illegal Immigrants Rounded Up in N.E. Sweep," *Boston Globe*, June 16, 2005.
7. Bob Port, Leslie Casimir, and Greg B. Smith, "Sex cons snared," *New York Daily News*, October 3, 2003.
8. Madeleine Cosman, Ph.D., Esq., "Illegal Aliens and American Medicine," *Journal of American Physicians and Surgeons*, Volume 10, Number 1, Spring 2005.
9. Quoted in "Immigration and Citizenship," by Edward J. Erler, Claremont Institute.
10. Cosman, "Illegal Aliens and American Medicine."
11. *Lou Dobbs Tonight*, Cable News Network (CNN), March 31, 2005.
12. CQ Transcriptions, news conference, Tony Blair, August 5, 2005.
13. "The Rekindled Flame," *Wall Street Journal*, July 3, 1990.
14. Michael Walzer, "What Does It Mean to Be an American?" *Social Research*, October 1, 2004.
15. Matthew Brock, "It's not the job, it's the wages," letter to the editor, *Arizona Republic*, October 25, 2005.

16. Luis Alberto Urrea, "America's bounty for Mexico," *Arizona Republic*, June 12, 2005.
17. Tony Brown, "Becoming a Republican," *Wall Street Journal*, August 5, 1991.
18. Jerry Kammer, "Grass Roots, Politicians Differ on Immigration," *Arizona Republic*, February 14, 2002.

INDEX